THE

# plant-based family

COOKBOOK

# THE
# plant-based
# family
## COOKBOOK

## 60
### Easy & Nutritious Vegan Meals
### Kids Will Love!

## Claire Swift & Sarah Biagetti
FOUNDERS OF HEALTHY TWISTS

PAGE STREET
PUBLISHING CO.

PAGE STREET
PUBLISHING CO.

First published in 2021 by

Page Street Publishing Co.

27 Congress Street, Suite 105

Salem, MA 01970

www.pagestreetpublishing.com

Distributed by Macmillan, sales in Canada by The Canadian Manda Group.

25  24  23  22  21   1 2 3 4 5

ISBN-13: 978-1-64567-424-5

ISBN-10: 1-64567-424-X

Library of Congress Control Number: 2021931968

Cover and book design by Rosie Stewart for Page Street Publishing Co.

Photography by Claire Swift

Food styling by Claire Swift & Sarah Biagetti

Printed and bound in the United States

Page Street Publishing protects our planet by donating to nonprofits like The Trustees, which focuses on local land conservation.

To all parents, you are doing an amazing job.
Keep going.

To our parents, for your kindness and
limitless love.

And to both our families, we'd be lost without
you. Pete, Nick, Aaron, Luca, Daniel, Matilda and
Louis, thank you for tolerating all the recipes in
development and for inspiring us to cook,
nourish and grow.

# Contents

# Introduction

Finding a meal that the whole family will eat, let alone enjoy, may feel like an impossible task. Fed up with the rejections? Tired of the constant bargaining and bribery, the toddler/teen tantrums or the anxiety from knowing that the food one family member will eat, another will point-blank reject?

Oh, we hear you! We've been there. You spend precious time lovingly cooking meals for your children, only for them to bluntly and often quite rudely refuse even to try them. So you watch it go cold, and are left feeling frustrated and defeated that you've wasted time and energy—don't even mention the food waste.

Like all parents, we know you have to pick your battles, choosing your timing carefully. This does not change as your children grow up. Then there are the breakthrough days, when suddenly broccoli is the favorite vegetable (peas are so last week). It may stay as the top vegetable for a couple of weeks and then they never want to see it again. But do not lose heart—always remember that this is a normal childhood behavior and will happen with whatever you feed your children. And if your partner, husband or wife makes any comment or rolls their eyes, just give them a little nudge under the table—they'll soon get the message.

A few years ago, we decided that it was time to address some of these challenges and at the same time we wanted our families to be eating and enjoying more plant-based food. That is what this book is all about—a collection of recipes to help you encourage your family to enjoy eating more plant-based meals.

Through the plant-based family recipes in this book, we hope that your children will become more confident and engaged eaters—children that are naturally prepared to try most new foods, flavors and meals without causing a fuss. This is a parenting achievement to be proud of.

This book is full of recipes that are delicious, wholesome, nourishing and easily achieved. It is an uncomplicated tool to use to introduce, gradually expand into or fully embrace a plant-based lifestyle.

In the beginning, we'd recommend making small changes—these might be adding a plant-based side dish to a meal or mixing more legumes and pulses into a meat-based dish. Other useful ideas are to start with a couple of fully plant-based meals a week, then do a whole day. Go on to add more days from there if that is your goal. Don't make a big fuss. If you just start including the ingredients and recipes, the family will be far less judgmental and more inclined to go with the flow.

## OUR FAMILIES AND FOOD

Five years ago, we launched our blog, Healthy Twists. We started writing as two friends with a slightly obsessive love of food and as a way for us to share recipes with family and friends. Since then, it has spiraled into food demonstrations, talks, magazine articles, events, photography and creating content for brands—filling our social media and website with tasty inspiration.

(continued)

We are home cooks; neither of us comes from foodie backgrounds or have any formal training. We started our careers in design and the arts, then we had children and decided it was time to learn how to feed them. We would walk miles with them in baby carrier backpacks and drink endless cups of tea while eating and discussing cakes together and herding the boys around the playgroups. It was during these moments that we realized our shared passion for food.

We'd discuss what food we'd much rather be eating and what we were going to eat next while laughing at the many times we'd been trying to soothe our babies and attempting to eat jam-covered toast that would then fall stickily in their baby hair.

As Sarah's second son arrived, her eldest became life-threateningly ill and was saved by a liver transplant at the age of two. From this point on, maintaining the health and well-being of our families became something of a crusade.

Over the years we have learned to nourish our families while balancing their health needs. Our recipes have to cater to life with a transplant and the lifelong taking of medication; genetic adult diabetes; childhood migraines; our own hormonal changes; gut health and the energy levels, growth and development of our rapidly changing children—plus add an older stepchild into this mix who is used to how another household eats. Like so many, we are constantly juggling with husbands who work long hours and are often traveling.

## HOW TO USE THIS BOOK

Our families, our own childhoods and the need for us to change the way we eat for the good of the planet, have helped define the values and purpose of Healthy Twists, and in turn set the aims for this cookbook.

As for all parents, our instinct is to support the growth and well-being of our children, and we hope this book will show how easy and tasty it is to eat more plant-based foods and to cook many from scratch. We want to inspire you to get creative in the kitchen and not to be afraid to switch up the recipe if you don't have the exact ingredients listed. Using what you have and improvising are two of our guiding principles.

Nearly all of the recipes are designed to have the option to be made both vegan *and* gluten-free. We have personally found that wheat can be a trigger food for IBS and that finding great vegan and gluten-free foods and recipes is almost impossible.

As families, we have definitely found that the children respond better to meals if we are all eating the same dish. We are aware that older children and adults may enjoy more seasoning, spice and heat in their food, though. So we always make sure there are chili flakes, fresh chilis and herbs for anyone to add to their meals if they would like.

We don't feel that this book is the place or platform to be preachy and pressure people into *going* "vegan/plant-based." We have never demanded that our children be plant-based—that's a decision for them to make. However, we hope that as you have picked up this particular recipe book, you are mindful of the impact eating meat, fish and dairy have on our beautiful and increasingly fragile planet. We also hope that through sharing these recipes with your family and friends, they, too, will be encouraged to try out more plant-based meals.

We have designed *The Plant-Based Family Cookbook* to cater to different cooking skill levels and different styles of planning—whether you do one weekly shopping trip or pick up ingredients throughout the week.

Finally, we have always advocated sharing the kitchen with children. By encouraging children from a very young age to be involved in the making of food, we have found they become more content eaters. Helping to mix cake batter, creating their own smoothie blends, learning to peel vegetables, leaving them to make simple dinners as they get older—these are all important life skills that we as parents have the privilege to share with our children. Admittedly that quick birthday cake may take a little longer to make when small hands are assisting, but this investment of time in them and their food will lead to them becoming adults who understand how to cook, where their ingredients come from and the importance of a balanced and nourishing way to eat.

Most of all, we want you to enjoy the recipes and find new family favorites. We look forward to seeing and hearing about the meals you and your family create from these pages. We'd love for you to share across social media using #healthytwistsfamilycookbook or message us on our website www.healthy-twists.com.

With love,

Claire & Sarah

# Glossary of Terms

This cookbook was written for an American audience, but to enable the recipes to be universally used, we have included a glossary of terms, as our community is across both sides of the Atlantic.

All milk, yogurt, butter, cream, crème fraîche, stock cubes and sauces included in or eaten with the recipes are vegan.

All recipes that can be made gluten-free give the gluten-free flour option in the ingredients.

## EQUIPMENT

Baking sheet/Sheet pan—Baking tray

Cake pan—Cake tin

Convection oven—Fan oven

Loaf pan—Loaf tin

Muffin papers—Muffin cases

Oven rack—Oven shelf

Skillet—Frying pan

## BAKING INGREDIENTS

All-purpose flour—Plain flour

Baking soda—Bicarbonate of soda

Confectioners' sugar—Icing sugar

Superfine caster sugar—Caster sugar

Molasses—Black treacle

## OTHER INGREDIENTS

Arugula—Rocket

Beets—Beetroot

Cilantro—Coriander

Corn—Sweetcorn

Ears of corn—Corn on the cob

Eggplant—Aubergine

Zucchini—Courgette

# Breakfast & Brunch

We love breakfast—it is one of the meals we think about the most. In fact, we start contemplating breakfast not long after we've finished our evening meal. Breakfast should be embraced, keenly anticipated and, when possible, allowed to create a moment of calm before the rest of the day unfolds. We aim for breakfast recipes that won't leave you hungry.

You may not feel that you are a "breakfast" person or family, but we looked at the impact on our families of not eating breakfast or eating the wrong breakfast. It quickly became apparent that starting the day the right way helps to balance blood sugar levels. This is key for helping stabilize hormonal changes, sustaining energy and attention spans throughout the day and even helping the diabetic and migraine sufferers in the family manage their symptoms.

In this chapter, we look beyond the mass-produced shop-bought breakfasts and cereals and delve into a vibrant world of deliciously healthy, easy and bright breakfasts created to bring joy to the start of your day. In the following pages, you will find a collection of nourishing breakfast recipes. Making them yourself means that you'll know exactly what ingredients are in them.

We love bowls of our Not Your Average Porridge (page 22), bubbling on the stove top for eight minutes, leaving you free to find your youngest's shoes. Just give the porridge a stir as you pass. You'll soon find you look forward to a bowl of porridge far more enthusiastically than you did a bowl of cold, bland air-filled cereal. For an extra treat, stir in a spoonful of the silky smooth Indulgent Homemade Chocolate Spread (page 21).

For weekend brunches, we can definitely recommend the Apple Waffles (page 18), the Breakfast Wraps (page 36) and the Tofu Scramble with Smoky Eggplant and Roasted Tomatoes (page 25). The recipes using silken tofu are a great protein boost and are the perfect accompaniment to a couple of tasty vegan sausages with sautéed mushrooms and a squeeze of sauce.

To keep your breakfast interesting all year round, make the most of the seasonal produce by varying the fruit you add to brighten your bowls. At the same time, one of our biggest top tips to help save money and food waste is to keep a freezer stash of frozen fruit for making quick compotes or whizzing into smoothies. We recommend mixed berries, blueberries, cherries, avocado and sliced banana—all so handy.

# Oat and Banana Pancakes

We know everyone has their go-to pancake recipe, but we find this recipe is one of the easiest ways to persuade our children to tuck into oats without realizing they are really having a healthy-ish breakfast—that is until they are let loose with the mix-and-match toppings. Our children ask for these pancakes time and time again.

The joy of this healthier pancake (made with oats blended into a flour and sweetened with banana, rather than made with all-purpose flour and refined sugar), is that it is quick to whip up a batch. On some mornings we'll eat half the batch and make the other half into pancakes for dessert with a scoop of ice cream. Or we'll save the batter in a container in the fridge for pancakes the next morning. Any leftover pancakes (an unlikely event) can be kept in an airtight container and reheated, too.

SERVES: 4 to 6    PREP TIME: 5 minutes    COOK TIME: 20 minutes to cook the whole batch

To make the pancake batter, in a blender, combine the oats, plant-based milk, water, apple cider vinegar, baking soda, vanilla extract and bananas. Then blend the ingredients until you have a fairly thick, smooth batter. If you would like to add any mix-ins, fold them into the batter with a spoon.

Heat a large nonstick skillet over medium to high heat and wipe a little oil over the base of the pan with some kitchen paper towels. Then use a tablespoon scoop to measure out the batter for each pancake directly into the pan. Cook the pancakes for about 3 minutes, until bubbles start to appear on the surface. Then turn them over to cook on the other side for another 3 minutes, until both sides are lightly golden. Repeat until all the batter is used up, remembering to wipe a little oil into the base of the pan in between each batch of pancakes.

If you want to keep the cooked pancakes warm until they are all cooked, place them onto a plate and put them into the oven on low heat until you are all ready to eat.

Enjoy your pancakes in a stack or spread a few on a plate with berries, maple syrup, sliced banana, melted chocolate or chocolate spread.

PANCAKES

*2 cups (180 g) rolled oats (gluten-free if needed)*

*1 cup (240 ml) unsweetened plant-based milk*

*½ cup (120 ml) water*

*1 tbsp (15 ml) apple cider vinegar*

*½ tsp baking soda*

*1 tsp vanilla extract*

*2 medium ripe bananas*

*Oil, for greasing*

OPTIONAL MIX-INS

*1 tbsp (15 ml) grade A maple syrup*

*½ cup (75 g) fresh blueberries*

*1 tbsp (16 g) nut butter*

*½ cup (85 g) vegan chocolate chips*

MIX-AND-MATCH TOPPINGS

*Sliced strawberries*

*Blueberries*

*Drizzle of maple syrup*

*Sliced banana*

*Drizzle of melted vegan chocolate*

*Indulgent Homemade Chocolate Spread (page 21)*

# Apple Waffles

Our families love waffles for breakfast. Ladling the batter onto the waffle iron, closing the lid, enjoying the sweet scent of them filling the kitchen and then biting into the crisp outside with the light, soft center—they are a real treat. These waffles use oats instead of flour as that is more sustaining, and we've added cooked apples to the waffle batter to create a lovely sweetness and texture.

The children enjoy the waffles as much for dessert as they do breakfast and have a cheeky habit of stacking them as they do their pancakes, layering them with berries and chocolate spread, with a final flourish of vegan whipped cream.

You will need a waffle maker or stove top waffle iron. We use a four-waffle electric waffle maker.

**MAKES:** 8 waffles    **PREP TIME:** 10 minutes    **COOK TIME:** 30 minutes

### WAFFLE MIX

*1½ cups (350 ml) unsweetened almond or oat milk*

*1 tbsp (15 ml) apple cider vinegar*

*2 apples, peeled and roughly chopped*

*⅓ cup (80 ml) water*

*1 tsp vanilla extract or ground cinnamon*

*2 cups (180 g) rolled oats (gluten-free if needed)*

*1 tbsp (14 g) coconut oil (solid), plus more for brushing the waffle iron*

*2 tsp (10 g) baking powder*

### TOPPING SUGGESTIONS

*Strawberries*

*Raspberries*

*Orange slices*

*Drizzle melted vegan dark chocolate*

*Drizzle grade A maple syrup*

*Indulgent Homemade Chocolate Spread (page 21)*

*Vegan whipped cream*

Pour the almond or oat milk into a small bowl and add the apple cider vinegar. Stir and set to one side.

Place the apples in a saucepan with the water and vanilla extract. Cook over medium heat for 10 minutes, until the apples have softened. Stir occasionally to prevent them from sticking to the base of the pan.

Once the apples have cooked, put them in a blender with the almond/oat milk mixture and the oats, coconut oil and baking powder. Then blend until the batter is smooth.

Heat the waffle iron and lightly brush it with coconut oil. Carefully spoon the waffle mix onto the hot waffle iron, spreading it out evenly. Close the lid and cook for 8 minutes. After 8 minutes, check the waffles and, if not completely golden, cook for a further 2 minutes.

Once the apple waffles are ready, place them on the table and let everyone help themselves to berries, orange slices, a drizzle of melted vegan chocolate or maple syrup, chocolate spread and vegan whipped cream.

# Indulgent Homemade Chocolate Spread

Making your own chocolate spread is a brilliant way to reduce the number of unnecessary hidden sugars in your children's food. Although we'd still class this silky spread as indulgent, it contains far less sugar than store-bought. This is delicious spread thickly onto toasted sourdough, stirred into porridge or spooned straight from the jar. We use a vegan dark chocolate with a minimum of 70 percent cocoa solids, or try with 85 percent cocoa solids for a really intense flavor.

The almond nut butter we use as the base for the spread is so easy to make and exactly the same process that we use to make all our own nut butters, using any nut or seed. We use 1 cup (140 g) of nuts to make a jar of nut butter.

MAKES: 125-ml jar    PREP TIME: 15 minutes    COOK TIME: 10 minutes

Preheat the oven to 325°F/160°C (150°C convection). Place the almonds onto a baking sheet and roast for 10 minutes. Remove the almonds from the oven and allow them to cool completely.

Meanwhile, melt the chocolate in a heatproof bowl resting on a saucepan of simmering water. Once the chocolate is melted, remove the bowl from the heat and add the oil, sugar, vanilla extract and a small pinch of salt, if using. Stir until combined.

Place the cooled almonds into a food processor and blend until they become a smooth nut butter. This may take up to 10 minutes, depending on the strength of the food processor. Now add the chocolate mix and blend together with the nut butter until smooth and silky.

Pour into a clean jar, with a lid, and eat within 1 week. Store in a cool, dry location.

1 cup (140 g) almonds

8 oz (226 g) dark vegan chocolate

3 tbsp (45 ml) extra-virgin olive oil

1 tbsp (15 g) golden superfine caster sugar

1 tsp vanilla extract

Pinch salt (optional)

# Not Your Average Porridge

For some, porridge is a seasonal breakfast—the first bowls being eaten as the temperature dips lower and the first morning frost appears. But for us, porridge and oats aren't a seasonal breakfast, as our bowls of porridge move in tune with the seasons. A wonderfully warm, nutritionally packed bowl of comfort food should be filled with changes in texture, pops of flavor and finished with some tasty toppings.

Creating a delicious and nutritious porridge isn't time-consuming and you can let go of any childhood fears of lumpy, solid or sloppy and tasteless bowls of gloop and let us guide you to creamy breakfast bowls of tasty goodness.

We'll start with how to make the porridge base and then share how to bring variety using layers of everyday staples and fresh seasonal ingredients. You will soon find that you are all eating porridge for breakfast all year round and no two days need be the same.

Variety is the best way to keep the children engaged. Simply set out a few bowls with different toppings, so that they can decorate or stick a smiley face on their porridge.

SERVES: 1     PREP TIME: 5 to 10 minutes     COOK TIME: 8+ minutes

PORRIDGE BASE

½ cup (45 g) rolled oats
(gluten-free if needed)

1 cup (240 ml) unsweetened
almond milk, oat milk or water

FLAVOR BOOSTS
(CHOOSE 1 TO 3)

1 tbsp (5 g) cacao powder

½ tsp vanilla extract

1 tbsp (15 ml) unsweetened vegan
coconut yogurt

½ tsp cinnamon powder

1 tbsp (9 g) mixed seeds—
pumpkin, sunflower, flax,
sesame, chia seeds

1 tsp nut butter—almond, peanut,
cashew or Indulgent Homemade
Chocolate Spread (page 21)

For the base porridge: Put the oats in a saucepan, pour over your choice of liquid and cook over medium heat for 6 to 8 minutes, stirring occasionally, until the oats are creamy and cooked to your desired consistency.

To elevate the base porridge: Put the oats and liquid into a bowl, mix, cover and then put into the fridge overnight. This will help make the oats easier to digest and save cooking time in the morning. Tip into the saucepan when you are ready to make your porridge.

Or put the oats and liquid in the pan and leave to soak for 30 minutes to make them extra creamy, then cook.

Stir in the flavor boosters: Once you have your base porridge, while you are cooking or soaking it, add 1 to 3 of the flavor boosts. We enjoy cacao powder + vanilla extract or yogurt + cinnamon—or just a tablespoon (9 g) of mixed seeds.

(continued)

FRUITY ADDITIONS

¼ cup (30–40 g) berries (blueberries, strawberries, raspberries, cherries or currants—use fresh or frozen)

½ banana, sliced or mashed

Zest of ½ lemon

1 dried date or apricot, chopped

Slices of apples or pears

BERRY COMPOTE

1 cup (154 g) frozen cherries or any frozen berry mix

1 tbsp (15 ml) grade A maple syrup

TASTY TEXTURED TOPPINGS

Vegan chocolate, 70%+ cacao solids (chunks, chips or buttons)

1 heaped tsp cacao nibs

Small handful granola, such as Cinnamon and Pecan Granola (page 31)

Small handful chopped nuts (almonds, pecans, walnuts, Brazils, cashews or hazelnuts)

1 tbsp (9 g) seeds (one type or a mix of pumpkin, sunflower, flax, sesame and chia seeds)

Small handful coconut chips or desiccated coconut

Good dollop unsweetened vegan yogurt (coconut, almond or other)

1 tsp nut butter for drizzling

**Stir in the fruity additions:** Add blueberries, cherries or half a mashed banana. Cooking the berries with the oats releases more of the berries' nutritional benefits, adds those beautiful pops of flavor and often turns the porridge pink or purple.

**To make a quick berry compote:** Simply put the frozen berries in a small skillet, pour over the maple syrup and cook over low to medium heat for 6 to 8 minutes. Stir regularly and the fruit will soften and become a jam-like consistency. Remove the pan from the heat, and the compote is ready to spoon onto your porridge. We regularly use different mixed frozen berries to make quick compotes to eat with our porridge. Make extra and store in a jar in the fridge for up to 3 days.

**Add any tasty textured toppings:** Spoon the porridge into a bowl and either keep it simple with the flavor combination you already have or try adding an additional topping for texture. For instance, break up a piece of dark chocolate, sprinkle the pieces over the porridge, watch it melt and stir it through. Granola is another brilliant addition to porridge, as it adds crunch along with lots of flavor.

# Tofu Scramble with Smoky Eggplant and Roasted Tomatoes

Tofu scramble is the tastiest plant-based alternative to scrambled eggs. Tofu has a satisfying bounciness and it is quick to soak up the flavors of the ingredients around it, making it perfect for adding a selection of vegetables, herbs and spices to it. In this tofu scramble we have used red bell peppers, spinach, spring onions and a little garlic, but we frequently vary the vegetables depending on the season or what's in the fridge. We've found that mixing different vegetables into the scramble is a great way of introducing new flavors to the children. The smoky eggplant slices complement the flavors of the scramble and the sweet roasted tomatoes. It's perfect for weekend brunches, lazy days or a light lunch.

SERVES: 4    PREP TIME: 15 to 20 minutes    COOK TIME: 20+ minutes

**To make the smoky eggplant slices:** Preheat the oven to 320°F/160°C (160°C convection) and line a large baking sheet with parchment paper.

Cut the eggplant in half down the middle, then slice each piece in half again so you have four quarters. Slice each piece of eggplant into thin slices no more than ¼ inch (0.5 cm) thick.

In a bowl, combine the soy sauce, Worcestershire sauce, olive oil, maple syrup, smoked paprika, garlic powder, salt and pepper and whisk together. Place the eggplant slices onto the lined baking sheet in a single layer and brush each slice generously with the marinade. Bake in the oven for 20 minutes.

(continued)

### SMOKY EGGPLANT SLICES

*1 small eggplant, thinly sliced*

*2 tbsp (30 ml) soy sauce or tamari*

*1 tbsp (15 ml) vegan Worcestershire sauce*

*1 tbsp (15 ml) extra-virgin olive oil*

*1 tbsp (15 ml) grade A maple syrup*

*1 tsp smoked paprika*

*¼ tsp garlic powder*

*Pinch salt*

*Freshly ground black pepper*

# Tofu Scramble with Smoky Eggplant and Roasted Tomatoes (Continued)

**To make the tofu scramble:** Drain the tofu in a sieve and set to one side. Pour the oil into a large skillet over medium heat. Add the spring onions and diced bell pepper to the pan and cook for 3 minutes until they start to soften. Then add the garlic and cook for another 3 minutes. Place the tofu into the pan with the vegetables and break it down with the back of a fork. Stir together, add the spinach and ground turmeric and heat through for 3 minutes until the spinach has wilted. Season to taste.

**To make the pan-fried tomatoes:** Add the olive oil to a skillet and bring to medium heat. Add the tomatoes and pan-fry for 5 minutes, until they start to become golden.

Divide the scrambled tofu among thick slices of sourdough toast topped with slices of smoky eggplant and sweet pan-fried cherry tomatoes.

### TOFU SCRAMBLE

*12 oz (340 g) organic silken tofu*

*1 tbsp (15 ml) extra-virgin olive oil*

*2 spring onions, finely diced*

*1 red bell pepper, diced*

*1 clove garlic, crushed and sliced*

*1 cup (30 g) spinach, roughly chopped*

*¼ tsp turmeric powder*

*Pinch salt*

*Freshly ground black pepper*

### PAN-FRIED TOMATOES

*1 tbsp (15 ml) extra-virgin olive oil*

*9 oz (250 g) cherry tomatoes or small vine tomatoes*

### TO SERVE

*Thick slices of sourdough bread, toasted and spread with vegan butter*

# Family-Friendly Smoothies

We lose count of how many smoothies we make in a week. Whether thick or thin, fruity or earthy blends, there are so many variations. Sometimes they are an addition to the breakfast spread or even the main breakfast, and other times a boosting after-school pick-me-up. We've found that with our children, smoothies are one of the easiest ways to add extra fruit, veg, fiber and nutrition into their day. You'll soon find that they will be making up their own flavor combinations.

These are the smoothie recipes that we make on regular rotation: the subtly flavored Super Green, an enticing and bright Vibrant Berry and our go-to chocolate fix The Choc-tastic. They are a great introduction to homemade smoothies, helping you to get the right ingredient ratio. For those of you who are experienced smoothie makers, they might give you a few more ideas.

We fully encourage you to embrace seasonal ingredients, mix up the vegetables and grains and add ingredients like fresh ginger to give you a digestive boost and a tasty kick to your smoothie. We use high-powered blenders. If yours is not as powerful, add a little more liquid to help the smoothies along.

You can make the smoothie-making process quicker by bagging up the smoothie mixes and freezing them. Then, simply remove one from the freezer, add it to the blender, pour over the liquid and blend.

---

**SERVES:** 1    **PREP TIME:** 5 minutes

---

### SUPER GREEN

½–1 small avocado or ¼ zucchini

½ apple or pear

½ cup (15 g) spinach

1 tbsp (9 g) pumpkin seeds

¾ cup (180 ml) unsweetened plant-based milk

### VIBRANT BERRY

½ cup (70 g) mixed frozen berries (blueberries, cherries or raspberries)

½–1 banana

1 tsp nut butter (peanut, almond or cashew)

1 heaped tbsp (15 ml) unsweetened vegan coconut yogurt

¾ cup (180 ml) unsweetened plant-based milk

### THE CHOC-TASTIC

1 tbsp (5 g) rolled oats (gluten-free if needed)

1 tbsp (5 g) cacao powder

½–1 banana

1 date, pitted

1 tsp nut butter

¾ cup (180 ml) unsweetened plant-based milk

### OPTIONAL ADDITIONS

Small piece fresh ginger

1 tsp mixed seeds

1 tbsp (15 ml) unsweetened vegan coconut yogurt

¼ cup (31 g) cucumber or zucchini

Put the ingredients for your chosen variation, along with any additions, into a high-powered blender. Pour over your choice of plant-based milk and whizz until you have a silky-smooth smoothie.

Pour into your glass and serve.

# Cinnamon and Pecan Granola

We think everyone should have a delicious granola recipe on hand. We always have a jar or two of different kinds that we make on repeat. This recipe is packed with goodness and tastes amazing for breakfast or as an afternoon snack. Granola is an incredibly satisfying breakfast and making it yourself is cheaper and ridiculously easy. Once made, granola is our go-to time-saver breakfast.

Enjoy with hot cinnamon milk in the colder months or with berries and yogurt in the summer. Toasting the ingredients releases lots of gorgeous flavors and is sweetened with a lovely combination of cinnamon and pecans. Toasted coconut flakes and gooey apricots provide a fiber boost.

If you do not like an ingredient, then switch it for one you do. Swap the same quantity of apricots for dates or cranberries. If you've run out of pumpkin seeds, add the same quantity of almonds, walnuts or pre-toasted buckwheat groats. Exchange the cinnamon for vanilla extract—make this recipe your own.

**MAKES:** Approx. 2.5 lbs (1 kg)     **PREP TIME:** 10 minutes     **COOK TIME:** 30 minutes

Preheat the oven to 325°F/160°C (150°C convection) and line a large baking sheet with parchment paper.

In a large mixing bowl, stir together the rolled oats, pecans, seeds and sea salt. In a large saucepan over low heat, gently melt together the coconut oil, maple syrup, vanilla extract and ground cinnamon. Once the coconut oil is melted, slowly add the oat-and-nut mixture to the pan and gradually mix together so everything is coated.

Carefully tip the granola onto the baking sheet and spread it out evenly to roughly ½-inch (1.5-cm) depth.

Place in the middle of the oven and bake for 30 minutes, or until golden brown.

Remove from the oven and allow the granola to cool completely. Now sprinkle over the roughly chopped apricots and toasted coconut flakes and mix them into the granola base.

Store in a sealed jar and use within a month.

*4 cups (360 g) rolled oats (gluten-free if needed)*

*2 cups (220 g) pecans, roughly chopped*

*⅔ cup (92 g) pumpkin seeds*

*⅔ cup (90 g) sunflower seeds*

*½ tsp sea salt*

*½ cup (100 g) coconut oil, solid*

*½ cup (120 ml) grade A maple syrup*

*2 tsp (10 ml) vanilla extract*

*1 tbsp (8 g) ground cinnamon*

*1 cup (160 g) dried unsulphured apricots, roughly chopped*

*1 cup (50 g) coconut flakes (we buy the kind that comes pre-toasted)*

# Mushroom, Spinach, Pesto and "Cheese" Toasted Sandwich

We love a quick toasted sandwich. Here we've elevated the traditional grilled cheese toastie into a brilliant breakfast sandwich with layers of pesto (page 45), mushrooms, spinach and melted "cheese." It's perfect for breakfast or a quick lunch, and you can enjoy all of these tasty fillings either piled onto a thick slice of toast or stuffed in a delicious savory toasted sandwich. For younger children who might find mushrooms and spinach a little overwhelming, start by spreading the bread with pesto, adding the cheese and maybe a few sliced mushrooms.

The toasties can easily be made using a griddle or a skillet—simply lightly oil the griddle or pan and place the sandwich on it. Cook on each side for 4 minutes, pressing down with a spatula as it cooks. We use a panini maker for our toasted sandwiches—we've had it over 10 years and it's a brilliant bit of kit.

SERVES/MAKES: 2    PREP TIME: 5 to 10 minutes    COOK TIME: 10 minutes

1 tbsp (15 ml) extra-virgin olive oil

7 oz (200 g) mushrooms, sliced

1 clove garlic, crushed and sliced

2 cups (60 g) spinach

4 slices sourdough

2 tbsp (30 ml) pesto (page 45)

1 cup (110 g) vegan cheese, grated

Ketchup or your favorite sauce, for serving

Pour the oil in a skillet over medium heat, then tip in the mushrooms and garlic. Cook for 4 minutes before adding the spinach. Continue to cook for a couple of minutes until the spinach has wilted.

To assemble the toastie, spread one side of each piece of bread with pesto, then place two slices of bread on the cooking surface, pesto-side up. Divide the mushroom mixture between the two slices, sprinkle over the vegan cheese and place the other slices of bread on top. Toast for 4 to 5 minutes, until the cheese is oozing and the bread is golden. Enjoy with your favorite sauce— we love tomato ketchup.

# Savory Buckwheat Galettes

We first discovered this mouthwatering dish a few years ago at our local market, where a young, culinarily gifted French couple filled the air with the scent of baking galettes. French galettes are a type of pancake made with buckwheat flour, which adds a lovely nutty taste. Our taste buds tingle just thinking about it; sadly, they returned to France, and we have been recreating our version of the galette ever since. Having an easy galette recipe means you can enjoy adding your own tasty fillings, but this recipe is our favorite. The savory galettes are wrapped around salty vegan Greek-style cheese, arugula, chopped walnuts and a sweet balsamic-maple drizzle. They are utterly irresistible. These galettes are a brilliant alternative to a slice of bread when you want something savory, too. Our children also love a sweet, filled version of the galette spread with our Indulgent Homemade Chocolate Spread (page 21) and loaded with berries.

**MAKES:** 4 to 6 galettes     **PREP TIME:** 10 minutes     **COOK TIME:** 10 to 15 minutes

**To make the drizzle:** In a small bowl whisk together the balsamic vinegar with the maple syrup.

**To make the galettes:** Sieve the flour, baking powder and salt into a mixing bowl. Pour in the unsweetened almond milk and the apple cider vinegar and whisk until you have a smooth batter.

Heat a little oil (½ teaspoon per galette) in a small nonstick skillet over medium to high heat. Then, in the center of the pan, pour about ½ cup (120 ml) of batter, swirling the pan as you go, until you have enough batter to coat the base. Cook for 2 to 3 minutes on the first side, until you can see the edges start to slightly lift away from the pan, then flip the galette and cook for a minute or so on the other side.

**To add the filling:** Once the galette has cooked, crumble over the cheese, add a few leaves of arugula, scatter over the walnuts and drizzle on a little of the dressing. Fold over the edges and carefully transfer to a plate. Repeat with the remaining batter— to speed up the process we often have two skillets on the go.

MAPLE-BALSAMIC DRIZZLE
*3 tbsp (45 ml) balsamic vinegar*
*1 tbsp (15 ml) grade A maple syrup*

GALETTES
*1¼ cups (150 g) buckwheat flour*
*½ tsp baking powder*
*Pinch salt*
*1⅔ cups (400 ml) unsweetened almond milk*
*1 tbsp (15 ml) apple cider vinegar*
*Extra-virgin olive oil, for the skillet*

FILLING
*7 oz (200 g) vegan Greek-style cheese or plant-based cheddar*
*1½ cups (45 g) arugula*
*¾ cup (90 g) walnuts, roughly chopped*

# Breakfast Wraps

A weekend breakfast deserves a little more attention than the Monday-to-Friday routine eats. These breakfast wraps are bursting with flavors that are all encased in one tasty roll. The wraps are packed full of creamy avocado, cooked mushrooms, our tofu scramble, grated vegan cheese, peppers and fresh spinach leaves, creating an easy, vibrant and healthy start to any weekend.

On the weekends, we often find ourselves watching our children play football or at a rowing regatta and these activities have early starts. We make the breakfast wraps the night before so that we can take them along and feed them to our ravenous children during or after an event.

MAKES: 4    PREP TIME: 10 minutes    COOK TIME: 15 to 20 minutes

## TOFU SCRAMBLE

12 oz (340 g) organic silken tofu

1 tbsp (15 ml) extra-virgin olive oil

½ red onion, finely diced

1 clove garlic, finely chopped

½ tsp paprika

¼ tsp ground turmeric

Pinch salt

Freshly ground black pepper

## MUSHROOMS

1–2 tbsp (15–30 ml) extra-virgin olive oil

5 oz (142 g) mushrooms, sliced

1 clove garlic, finely chopped

1 tbsp (15 ml) soy sauce or tamari

## WRAP FILLINGS

4 whole wheat wraps or flatbreads (page 77)

Fresh spinach leaves

½ red bell pepper, sliced

1 avocado, sliced

1 cup (110 g) vegan cheese, grated

**To prepare the tofu:** Drain the tofu in a sieve and set to one side. To remove any excess water from the tofu, press it with some kitchen paper towels.

**To cook the mushrooms:** Place a skillet over medium heat and pour in the olive oil. Tip in the sliced mushrooms and cook for 5 minutes, until they start to soften. Add the garlic and soy sauce and cook for 2 more minutes. Keep the mushrooms warm while you prepare the tofu scramble.

**To make the tofu scramble:** Pour the olive oil into a large skillet over medium heat. Add the onion and garlic, then stir and cook for 4 minutes, until they start to soften. Now crumble in the tofu, breaking up any large pieces of tofu with a spatula, and sprinkle over the paprika and ground turmeric. Stir into the tofu and heat through for 6 minutes. Season to taste with salt and pepper.

**To fill the breakfast wrap:** Spread out a wrap, add some spinach to the center, a spoonful of mushrooms, some tofu scramble, a few slices of red bell pepper and avocado and a sprinkle of grated cheese. Carefully roll, then slice each wrap into four pieces. These are best when eaten fresh.

# Lunch Times

If you asked us to choose one of these tasty lunchtime recipes over another, we couldn't. We make them all regularly and often double batch so that they can be enjoyed for lunch the following day. These recipes are also ideal for a lighter dinner choice, too.

Our jobs mean that we predominantly work from home, but it wasn't always that way. We've had many uninspiring lunchtimes at our desks, so we know that it is very easy to get stuck in a lunchtime rut. There is the grabbing a lackluster sandwich, something with toast, crackers or dunking a carrot stick into a pot of hummus—the alternative is spending a fortune and buying lunch every day. The same can happen with the kids' school-packed lunches, which often become repetitive. We feel that with a bit of conscious planning and these recipes, you can avoid all of that and have nutritious, delicious lunches instead. Working these recipes into our weekly routine keeps the whole family's taste buds satisfied and stops our stomachs from growling.

Check out the Chickpea "Tuna" Sandwich filling (page 41), which also partners brilliantly with a baked potato or as part of a salad box. Some of these lunchtime recipes may take a few more minutes to prepare than a sandwich, but those minutes can be the difference that helps maintain everyone's afternoon productivity and avoid the 3:00 p.m. energy slump. Besides, if we are honest with ourselves, we'd all prefer a lunch we are looking forward to and not just going through the motions of eating.

Several of the recipes are as tasty cold as they are hot. The Kale, Leek and Potato Pastries (page 49) have to be tried to be believed—so simple to make and the flavor combination will have any kale skeptics converted. And try the Chickpea Omelette (page 42); it is ridiculously good!

The children will enjoy the creamy homemade Green Pesto with Butter Beans and Pasta (page 45). We always have a jar of pesto in the fridge, since this is a quick, versatile recipe that is a delicious addition to many different dishes. The vibrant Spinach Crêpes (page 50) will surprise them, too. Our kids use them like wraps and stuff them full of vegan cream cheese and grated carrots or leftover Three-Bean Chili (page 85).

Importantly, always remember that leftovers make brilliant lunches, so it's often worth creating more than you need for the meal and packing it for school or work the next day. Many of the recipes from Quick and Easy Mid-Week Meals (page 53), Batch Cooking and Freezer Meals (page 81) and the Oven to Table (page 97) chapters will make brilliant lunches. Our children have insulated food flasks and filling these with a tasty hot meal in the colder months makes a delicious alternative to a cold packed lunch.

# Chickpea "Tuna" Sandwich

This is a tasty plant-based take on tuna salad. We've used the humble chickpea, which is an amazing, nutritionally packed and versatile ingredient to always have in your pantry. Here we've transformed chickpeas into a super quick and easy lunchtime sandwich filling.

In just a few minutes, you'll have a family-friendly lunch prepared, perfect for adding to sandwiches, into pitas, on crackers or as a gorgeous filling for a baked potato. You can add any extras that you like, but we suggest bell peppers for some crunch, olives for a burst of saltiness or corn for a classic combination.

**SERVES: 2    PREP TIME: 10 minutes**

Drain and rinse the chickpeas before placing them into a mixing bowl. Use the back of a fork or a potato masher to mash them to your desired consistency. Alternatively, use a food processor to pulse the ingredients together—we like to leave the chickpeas slightly chunky and not completely smooth.

Add the mayonnaise, lemon juice, Dijon mustard, capers, salt and pepper and mix together until combined. Then stir in the dill or parsley.

You may also like to add or stir in any of the optional additions to your chickpea "tuna" filling. The filling is now ready to spread onto slices of bread with lettuce.

Store any remaining filling in an airtight container in the fridge for up to 2 days.

1 (14-oz [400-g]) can chickpeas, drained (reserve the liquid for Summer Berry Meringues on page 141)

3 tbsp (45 ml) vegan mayonnaise

Juice of ¼ lemon

½ tsp Dijon mustard

2 tbsp (15 g) capers, roughly chopped

Pinch salt

¼–½ tsp freshly ground black pepper

Small handful dill or parsley, finely chopped

4 slices bread

Lettuce

OPTIONAL ADDITIONS

½ cup (70 g) corn

¼ cup (30 g) vegan grated cheese

1 red or green bell pepper, diced

¼ cup (45 g) black or green olives

3 spring onions, sliced

½ tsp chili flakes

# The Chickpea Omelette

The inspiration for this chickpea flour omelette comes from the Italian recipe for *farinata*. This simple and delicious dish has a wonderful Mediterranean taste and scent created by the combination of the chickpea flour, extra-virgin olive oil and rosemary. Traditionally eaten on its own, this naturally gluten-free, plant-based recipe allows you to vary the ingredients you add to it, making it the perfect seasonal lunch. The recipe is incredibly easy to make and the mix is infused with fresh rosemary. The gram (chickpea) flour gives this omelette its unique texture—soft on the inside and lightly crisp and golden on the outside.

We'd recommend whisking together the four batter ingredients the evening before (or at breakfast time), so that the chickpea omelette is ready to make. To speed up the cooking process, use more than one ovenproof skillet at a time (if you have them) to make more than one omelette at a time. Slice a cooked omelette into six pieces and share.

SERVES: 4    PREP TIME: 5 minutes plus 4+ hours inactive    COOK TIME: 15 minutes per omelette

*11 oz (315 g) gram flour (chickpea flour)*

*4 cups plus 2 tbsp (1 L) warm water*

*1 tsp baking powder*

*½ cup (120 ml) extra-virgin olive oil, plus more for the skillet*

*Pinch salt*

*Freshly ground black pepper*

*2 tbsp (4 g) fresh rosemary leaves*

FILLING SUGGESTIONS
*Cooked rosemary potatoes with roasted red peppers*

*Stir-fried kale and toasted pine nuts*

*Vegan feta cheese, peas and fresh mint*

*Sun-dried tomatoes and spring onions*

In a large bowl, whisk together the flour, water, baking powder and oil until you have a smooth batter. Then cover and leave the batter to rest at room temperature for at least 4 hours (or you could let it rest overnight if needed).

When you are ready to cook the omelette, remove any foam that may have formed on top with a spoon. Add the salt and pepper to the batter and whisk together.

Preheat the oven to 400°F/200°C (180°C convection). Place a 9-inch (22-cm) ovenproof skillet over medium heat and pour in a little oil. Add a little of the chopped rosemary to the oil and fry for 30 seconds to let it infuse. Then pour in 1½ cups (350 ml) of batter and swirl it around the pan; it should be about ¼ inch (5 mm) thick. Cook for 5 minutes, until the batter starts to bubble. If you are including any of the filling suggestions, add them to the batter in the pan at this point. Then transfer the skillet to the oven and cook the omelette for 8 to 10 minutes, or until the top turns golden in color and the edges are starting to crisp and come away from the sides of the pan.

Transfer the cooked omelette to a plate and, if not eating straight away, keep it warm by covering the plate with foil. Before cooking the next omelette, be sure to add a little more oil to the pan. Then repeat the steps with more batter until it's all used up.

Serve immediately, either whole or cut like pizza slices. Any remaining batter will store in a container in the fridge for up to 24 hours. Any leftover omelettes will keep covered for up to 2 days in the fridge.

# Green Pesto with Butter Beans and Pasta

From the moment our children could eat nuts, pesto has been part of their foodie lives, and we know that a delicious meal is never far away if we have a jar of pesto in the fridge. Making your own pesto is quick and easy and adds so much flavor to your food. It lifts the flavor of pasta dishes, is seriously tasty stirred through bean salads and spread onto toast, and is great in sandwiches or as a pizza topping. This is a mixed-leaf pesto recipe and we've used fresh basil leaves and spinach; we've also switched the usual pine nuts for walnuts or almonds, as they create a creamier pesto. The pesto will keep in the fridge for a week or can be frozen in an ice cube tray—this is really handy.

Use the ingredient ratios of this pesto recipe to experiment with different herbs or seasonal salad leaves. Wild garlic, kale and arugula leaves all make amazing pesto and using a good quality extra-virgin olive oil elevates their flavors. We like to toast the nuts, as that brings extra flavor to the pesto, but this step can be optional if you are pushed for time.

SERVES: 4 and makes 7 oz (200 g) of pesto     PREP TIME: 10 minutes     COOK TIME: 15 minutes

**To make the pesto: Heat a dry skillet over medium to high heat. Add the nuts and lightly toast them for 4 minutes; move the nuts occasionally so that they do not burn. Allow them to cool for a few minutes.**

**Add the toasted nuts, spinach, basil, garlic, lemon juice, nutritional yeast, extra-virgin olive oil, salt and pepper to a food processer and blend until the ingredients become a slightly rough paste.**

**To make the pasta and butter beans: In a large saucepan, cook the pasta according to the package instructions. Reserve a little of the cooking water in a small bowl, then drain the pasta and drain and rinse the butter beans. Return both to the pan the pasta was cooked in.**

**Heat the pan over medium heat, add 4 tablespoons (60 ml) pesto and stir until all the butter beans are warmed through and all the ingredients are generously coated in the pesto. If the pasta looks a little thick, stir in an extra drizzle of oil or a splash of the pasta water to loosen.**

**To serve: Add the chopped tomatoes and a few fresh basil leaves, stir them in and serve.**

NOTE: *You can keep the pesto in a sealed jar in the fridge for a week. Remember to drizzle a little oil over the pesto before sealing the jar to keep it from oxidizing.*

## PESTO
*⅓ cup (50 g) walnuts or almonds*

*1 cup (30 g) fresh spinach*

*1¼ cups (30 g) fresh basil*

*1 clove garlic, crushed*

*Juice of ½ lemon*

*2 tbsp (10 g) nutritional yeast*

*⅓ cup (80 ml) extra-virgin olive oil*

*½ tsp salt*

*1 tsp freshly ground black pepper*

## PASTA AND BUTTER BEANS
*2 cups (200 g) farfalle pasta (½ cup [50 g] per person; gluten-free if needed)*

*1 (13-oz [370-g]) can butter beans, drained*

## TOPPINGS
*1 cup (150 g) mixed roughly chopped tomatoes*

*Fresh basil*

# Pomegranate, Edamame Bean and Quinoa Super Salad

Gone are the days of thinking salad is wilting lettuce, soft cucumber and just a few slices of bedraggled tomato. This vibrant salad is packed full of tasty ingredients, filled with different textures, colorful vegetables and fresh herbs, with pops of pomegranate and juicy orange slices creating sweet and fresh flavors. The combination of nutty quinoa and wild rice is the perfect nutritious base for mixing with bell pepper, tomatoes, cucumber, edamame beans, mixed seeds and fruit. Enjoy drizzled with a refreshing olive oil and orange dressing.

This salad makes a stunning shared lunch and will retain its crunch and flavor in lunchboxes; it will also take pride of place in the middle of any barbecue or picnic table.

SERVES: 4 to 6    PREP TIME: 15 to 20 minutes    COOK TIME: 20 minutes

⅔ cup (100 g) mixed quinoa

½ cup (150 g) wild rice

8 stems broccoli

½ cup (155 g) edamame beans

4 oz (100 g) pomegranate seeds, plus a few for garnish

1 orange, peeled and cut into segments

½ cup (30 g) roughly chopped fresh parsley

3 tbsp (15 g) roughly chopped fresh mint leaves

1 red bell pepper, diced

½ cucumber, chopped into small pieces

1 cup (149 g) cherry tomatoes, halved

3 medium carrots, grated

⅓ cup (45 g) mixed seeds

## ORANGE SALAD DRESSING

¾ cup (180 ml) extra-virgin olive oil

Juice of 2 oranges

¼ cup (60 ml) white wine vinegar

Pinch salt

Freshly ground black pepper

Cook the quinoa and wild rice in separate pans according to the package instructions. Drain, rinse with cold water and set to one side.

Meanwhile, trim the broccoli stems. Bring a saucepan of salted water to a boil, then add the broccoli and edamame beans. Cook for 4 minutes, then drain.

To make the dressing, whisk together the olive oil, orange juice, vinegar, salt and pepper in a small bowl or jar.

Before mixing the salad ingredients together, put a handful of pomegranate seeds, a few slices of orange and herb leaves to one side.

Assemble the salad in a large serving bowl. Tip in the cooked quinoa and rice and add the broccoli, edamame beans, bell pepper, cucumber, tomatoes, carrots and seeds with the pomegranate seeds, orange segments and herb leaves and carefully mix together. Finally, scatter over the reserved pomegranate seeds, slices of orange and herb leaves. When the salad is ready to serve, drizzle over the orange and olive oil dressing.

The undressed salad will keep in a container in the fridge for up to 2 days. The dressing will keep in a sealed jar in the fridge for up to 2 days—shake to liven it back up again.

# Kale, Leek and Potato Pastries

These golden baked savory pastries are filled with comforting flavors. Don't be fooled by the simplicity of the ingredients in this recipe; when combined they create a mouthwateringly satisfying lunch. You will not be able to resist them straight from the oven, and they are equally tasty cold, when they make a great addition to a lunch box or picnic.

Younger taste buds aren't often fans of kale, but we find that kale wrapped in the other flavors means that the whole family devours these pastries and always demands more.

Before buying the chilled pastry, check that the ingredients are plant-based. We always have a pack of ready-made pastry in the freezer. It is a really handy base ingredient for savory recipes like the Asparagus, Potato and Pea Open Tart (page 73).

**MAKES:** 6    **PREP TIME:** 20 minutes    **COOK TIME:** 35 minutes

Preheat the oven to 400°F/200°C (180°C convection). Line a large baking sheet with parchment paper.

Bring a large saucepan of water to a boil and add the potatoes. Cook them for about 10 minutes, until just tender. Drain the potatoes and set aside to cool.

Add 1 tablespoon (15 ml) of oil to a medium skillet over medium heat. Then add the finely sliced leek and cook for 8 minutes, until it starts to soften. Now add the kale and lemon zest and continue to cook for 3 minutes, until the kale is cooked. Remove from the heat.

In a large bowl, combine the cooked potatoes, leek, kale, grated cheese, salt, pepper and the remaining tablespoon (15 ml) of olive oil. Mix together, breaking some of the potatoes up a little, but making sure there are still some good bite-size pieces.

Remove the pastry from the packet and unroll onto the lined baking sheet. Spoon the filling lengthways along the pastry, about ¾ inch (2 cm) away from the edge and about 3½ inches (8 cm) in depth along the center line of the pastry.

Then, fold over the pastry, covering the filling until the edges meet. Seal by pressing the overlapping pastry edges together with a fork or your fingers. Cut the pastry roll into six equal pieces.

In a small bowl, mix together the plant-based milk and Worcestershire sauce. Brush the tops of the pastry pieces generously with the glaze and sprinkle with the sesame seeds.

Place in the oven on the middle rack and bake for 35 minutes until golden brown. Remove from the oven, leave to cool slightly and then take a flavor-filled bite.

To store, allow to cool fully, place in a container and store in the fridge for up to 2 days.

*1 lb (450 g) potatoes (about 3 medium), cut into 1-inch (2-cm) rough cubes*

*2 tbsp (30 ml) extra-virgin olive oil, divided*

*1 medium leek, finely sliced*

*1½ cups (100 g) kale, stalks removed and finely sliced*

*Zest of ½ lemon*

*¾ cup (80 g) vegan cheese, grated*

*Pinch salt*

*Freshly ground black pepper*

*1 (11-oz [ 320-g]) pack vegan puff pastry (gluten-free if needed)*

*1 tbsp (9 g) sesame seeds*

GLAZE
*2 tbsp (30 ml) unsweetened plant-based milk*

*1 tbsp (15 ml) vegan Worcestershire sauce*

# Spinach Crêpes

You may have noticed that our families love flatbreads, pancakes, galettes and crêpes. Although we do encourage our children to eat with cutlery 90 percent of the time, there are days when they are really tired and you just want them to eat an easy, no-fuss, nutritious meal. This is where these tasty, strangely green spinach crêpes sneak handily into our cooking repertoire.

We find the best way to serve these is to make the crêpes, pile them on a plate in the center of the table among the many filling options and allow the family to help themselves. For fillings, we've chosen homemade hummus spread thickly across the base and then topped with sliced tomatoes, salad leaves and fresh herbs—or the children also love vegan cream cheese.

SERVES: 4     PREP TIME: 10 minutes     COOK TIME: 25 minutes

### SPINACH CRÊPES
*2 cups (250 g) gram flour (chickpea flour)*

*2 cups (480 ml) unsweetened almond or oat milk*

*1⅔ cups (50 g) spinach*

*¼ cup (15 g) fresh parsley leaves*

*1 tsp apple cider vinegar*

*Pinch salt*

*Freshly ground black pepper*

*Extra-virgin olive oil*

### SUGGESTED CRÊPE FILLINGS
*Homemade hummus or vegan cream cheese*

*1 carrot, grated*

*Mixed salad leaves or chopped lettuce*

*Tomatoes, sliced*

Add the flour, milk, spinach, parsley, vinegar, salt and pepper to a blender or food processer and blend until you have a smooth batter. You can leave the batter to stand while you prepare your fillings.

Heat a medium skillet (we use one between 7 and 9 inches [18 to 22-cm]) over medium to high heat. Carefully wipe a little olive oil around the pan with some kitchen paper towels. Then, using ½ cup (120 ml) of batter, swirl the mix across the base of the pan. Fry for 3 to 4 minutes, until little bubbles start to form on the surface of the crêpe. Then, using a spatula, carefully flip the crêpe over and cook for another 3 to 4 minutes. Transfer the crêpe to a plate and repeat with the remaining batter, adding a little oil to the pan each time.

Serve the crêpes rolled up, folded in half or quarters or open and filled with hummus, grated carrot and salad leaves in the middle or cream cheese, grated carrot, chopped lettuce and tomatoes.

Wrap any remaining crêpes in foil and place them in the fridge for up to 24 hours.

# Quick and Easy Mid-Week Meals

As our family lives have become increasingly chaotic, our everyday meals have had to adapt. We still want them to be full of flavor, vibrant, nourishing and easy enough to make at the end of a long day. Throughout this chapter you will find many of our favorite recipes to cook and enjoy with our families—we are fairly sure we now cook them on autopilot, knowing them by heart. When we can, we cook from scratch, and this selection of quick and easy mid-week meals are designed to be made with minimum effort to achieve maximum flavor and satisfaction, all with reduced cleaning up.

Trying to remove an element of stress from mealtimes when you've had a busy day and the kids are tired, hungry and shouting, "When's dinner ready? I'm hungry!" is the aim of this chapter. We want mealtimes to be enjoyable, with everyone as relaxed as possible and ready to tuck in and enjoy their meal. This is made easier with recipes like the Crispy Tofu Nuggets (page 55). There are the Smoky Black Bean-Loaded Fajitas (page 59) that are perfect to arrange across the middle of the table, ready for everyone to have fun assembling themselves. When the children are small, eating together teaches them everything from table manners and cutlery skills to encouraging them to try foods they'd avoid (because they see you eat them, they will eat them, too). We've also found that as the children get older, they offer less information about their days, and one of the best ways to get them to relax and open up is to share meals around the table. We regularly find out far more than the children had planned to tell us.

Since our children were small, they have loved the nourishing Ramen Noodle Bowls (page 66), with warming flavorsome broth, fresh vegetables and soft noodles—ideal for the days when you need a quick meal that is pure, reassuring comfort in a bowl.

As parents, we all know that trying new flavors and textures with our children can sometimes be a challenge, but we have found that using ingredients that balance sweetness with warmth can smooth over the introduction. The perfect place to start may just be the Sweet Chili and Ginger Tofu with Vegetable Rice (page 70). Tofu is brilliant at absorbing flavors, so marinating the tofu first in the sweet chili and ginger adds fantastic flavor.

No quick and easy meal chapter would be complete without a pasta dish or two, and we've included our classic vegan twists on family favorites that will make you smile. Enjoy a lighter pasta bowl with a few simple ingredients for summer days, like the Zucchini and Pea Carbonara (page 69)—a creamy dish with pan-fried zucchini, fresh lemons and fresh parsley. We couldn't resist including our plant-based take on the classic: "meatballs" made with black beans, a simple tomato sauce and spaghetti (page 61) for a reassuringly familiar meal.

We know your family will enjoy these recipes as much as our families and children do.

# Crispy Tofu Nuggets with a Smoky Herb Coating

From experience, we know that children much prefer eating with their fingers and dipping bite-size food into sauce. These nutritious, crispy coated tofu nuggets with a lightly spiced herb crumb are delicious dunked in tomato sauce. The addition of sesame seeds gives the nuggets a nutty flavor and is also a great way to add extra fiber to the meal. We eat them with sweet potato fries and minted peas. They also taste great in a flatbread with crisp salad leaves and a lemon yogurt dressing.

SERVES/MAKES: 4 (makes approx. 18 nuggets)     PREP TIME: 15 minutes     COOK TIME: 30 minutes

Preheat the oven to 425°F/220°C (200°C convection) and line a medium baking sheet with parchment paper.

Drain the tofu and remove any excess moisture by pressing with kitchen paper towels. Slice the block of tofu into ½-inch (1-cm)-thick pieces or break into roughly 1-inch (2-cm) cube pieces.

Pour the unsweetened plant-based milk into a shallow bowl, then add the lemon juice and stir.

In a second shallow bowl, mix together the bread crumbs, sesame seeds, paprika, garlic powder, turmeric, mixed herbs and lemon zest with a pinch of salt and black pepper to taste.

Put the all-purpose flour in a third bowl.

To coat the tofu pieces, take a piece of tofu and place it in the plant-based milk and lemon juice mix, then roll in the flour and make sure it is fully covered. Then, lightly dunk it back in the liquid and finally into the bread crumb mixture, ensuring the tofu is fully coated. Put it on the lined baking sheet. Repeat this process with all the tofu pieces.

Place the baking sheet into the oven and bake for 20 minutes. After 20 minutes turn each piece of tofu over. Return the baking sheet to the oven to cook for a further 10 minutes. The tofu will turn a light golden color when ready. Serve with lemon wedges.

Store any remaining nuggets in an airtight container in the fridge for up to 24 hours.

*14 oz (400 g) organic firm tofu*

*⅓ cup (80 ml) unsweetened plant-based milk*

*Juice of ½ lemon*

*1 cup (108 g) bread crumbs (gluten-free if needed)*

*3 tbsp (30 g) sesame seeds*

*1 tsp paprika or smoked paprika*

*1 tsp garlic powder*

*¼ tsp turmeric powder*

*½ tsp mixed dried herbs*

*Zest of ½ lemon*

*Pinch salt*

*Freshly ground black pepper*

*½ cup (60 g) all-purpose flour (gluten-free if needed)*

*Lemon wedges, for serving*

# Green Mac and Cheese

The joy of this pasta dish is that it's filled with great green vegetables blended into a smooth sauce, so the only surprise is that the pasta is bright green, which younger children will find entertaining.

This is a brilliant way for the whole family to enjoy a plant-based version of the classic mac and cheese, but with the added health benefit that it is packed full of fiber. We've used a variety of green vegetables in this vibrant, creamy, ever-popular pasta dish.

We felt the recipe needed to be versatile. To that end, you can use the smooth creamy green sauce on its own for younger children or stir bonus steamed broccoli or peas and corn into the pasta for older children for added texture and a vegetable boost.

SERVES: 4    PREP TIME: 10 minutes    COOK TIME: 20 to 25 minutes

2 oz (55 g) vegan butter

1 medium leek, finely sliced

2 cloves garlic, crushed and finely chopped

2 tbsp (16 g) all-purpose flour (gluten-free if needed)

2 cups (480 ml) unsweetened plant-based milk

1 cup (134 g) frozen peas

3 cups (100 g) spinach

1–2 tbsp (5–10 g) nutritional yeast

2 tsp (5 g) mustard powder

Pinch salt

Freshly ground black pepper

1 cup (100 g) vegan cheese, grated, plus more for serving

Dried macaroni pasta or whole wheat pasta (2–3 oz [56–84 g] per person; gluten-free if needed)

OPTIONAL VEGETABLE ADDITIONS

9 oz (250 g) steamed broccoli

¼ cup (40 g) peas

¼ cup (40 g) corn

TO SERVE

Extra vegan cheese

Melt the butter in a large skillet over medium heat. Add the sliced leek and garlic and cook for 10 minutes, until softened, stirring regularly. Sprinkle over the flour and whisk into the leeks, then slowly pour in the plant-based milk, whisking regularly. Simmer for 5 minutes, until the sauce starts to thicken.

Add the peas, spinach, nutritional yeast, mustard powder, salt, pepper and vegan cheese to the sauce and stir through for 5 to 8 minutes, until the spinach has wilted. Carefully pour the sauce into a blender and blitz until it is silky-smooth. Return the sauce to the skillet and keep it warm over low heat while the pasta cooks.

Meanwhile, in a large saucepan cook the pasta according to the package instructions. If you have a steamer, use it to steam the broccoli (if using) over the pasta pan for 5 minutes. Drain the pasta and return it to the pan, then pour in enough green vegetable sauce to coat all the pasta to your liking. Stir over medium heat for a few minutes, then add the steamed broccoli florets and peas or corn (if using). Serve in bowls and sprinkle with more cheese.

Any remaining pasta sauce can be portioned into airtight containers and frozen or kept in the fridge for 2 days. Leftover green mac and cheese can be stored in a container in the fridge for the next day.

# Smoky Black Bean–Loaded Fajitas

Our children (and husbands) love smoky black beans, which is great as black beans are chock-full of so much goodness, a brilliant source of protein and high in fiber. These black beans are lightly spiced, but as the children grow, their palates will develop and you can gradually add a touch more spice. Our teenagers love a bit more of a kick to the black beans. We load the fajitas with the spiced black beans, a vibrant golden corn salsa and pan-fried peppers and onions that are then topped with avocado cream and a sprinkle of vegan cheese. Everything is parcelled into soft tortillas or our homemade flatbreads (page 77). The kids adore these—making an ideal meal for everyone to help themselves.

SERVES: 4    PREP TIME: 20 minutes    COOK TIME: 25 minutes

**To make the black beans:** Heat a skillet over medium heat, then add a splash of olive oil and the garlic and cook for 1 minute before adding the cinnamon, cumin and chipotle paste. Stir for another minute to gently toast the spices, then tip in the beans and their liquid. Bring to a simmer. Reduce the heat and cook for 10 to 15 minutes, until the liquid has thickened, but the beans are still holding their shape. Season with salt and pepper. If the beans look too thick, add a splash of water to loosen.

**To make the golden corn salsa:** Heat another skillet over medium heat, add the olive oil and tip in the corn. Turn the heat to high and cook for 5 minutes until the corn starts to char. Remove from the heat and set to one side to cool. Once cooled, put the corn in a mixing bowl and add the chopped tomatoes, cilantro, lime juice, salt and pepper. Stir until thoroughly combined.

(continued)

### BLACK BEAN FAJITA MIX

1 tbsp (15 ml) extra-virgin olive oil

1 clove garlic, sliced

1 tsp ground cinnamon

1 tsp ground cumin

¼–½ tsp chipotle paste (optional)

2 (13.5-oz [400-g]) cans black beans (retain the liquid)

Small pinch salt

Freshly ground black pepper

### GOLDEN CORN SALSA

1 tbsp (15 ml) extra-virgin olive oil

1 cup (136 g) corn

1 cup (150 g) cherry tomatoes, roughly chopped

Small handful cilantro, roughly chopped

Juice of ½ lime

Pinch salt

Freshly ground black pepper

# Smoky Black Bean–Loaded Fajitas (Continued)

**To make the peppers and onions:** Re-use the corn skillet and heat the olive oil over medium heat. Add the sliced onion and bell peppers and cook for 8 to 10 minutes, stirring regularly, until the vegetables are soft and starting to brown slightly. Add a splash of water if the pan gets too dry and the onion starts to stick.

**To make the avocado cream:** Scoop the flesh of the avocados into a blender with the coconut yogurt and lime juice. Blitz until smooth and creamy. Spoon into a bowl and set aside.

**To assemble:** Warm the tortillas through in a dry skillet over medium heat for a couple of minutes on each side and serve filled with the peppers and onions, black beans, avocado cream and corn salsa. Top with shredded vegan cheese and cilantro.

The black beans and the salsa will store in an airtight container in the fridge for 2 days.

## PEPPERS AND ONIONS
*1–2 tbsp (15–30 ml) extra-virgin olive oil*

*1 red onion, finely sliced*

*1 red bell pepper, sliced*

*1 yellow bell pepper, sliced*

## AVOCADO CREAM
*2 avocados*

*¼–½ cup (60–120 ml) unsweetened vegan coconut yogurt*

*Juice of ½ lime*

## TO SERVE
*Corn tortillas or flatbreads (page 77)*

*Shredded vegan cheese*

*Cilantro*

# Tasty Meat-Free Balls with Spaghetti

You can never go wrong with "meatballs." The kids have always loved them and so we know that this fail-safe recipe will be a big hit with your family. It's a great introduction to plant-based eating for younger children because meatballs and spaghetti are instantly recognizable.

The meatballs are made from a mix of black beans, herbs and spices. We've used oats instead of bread crumbs for an additional fiber boost. We've kept the tomato sauce light and simple and the combination with the spaghetti is a meal to keep a family happy.

**SERVES/MAKES:** 4 and makes 24 balls    PREP TIME: 15 minutes    COOK TIME: 35 minutes

**"MEATBALLS"**

1 medium red onion

3 cloves garlic

3 tbsp (32 g) tomato puree

Zest of 1 lemon

1½ tbsp (20 ml) soy sauce or tamari

1½ tbsp (20 ml) balsamic vinegar

3½ cups (600 g) canned black beans, drained

¾ cup (75 g) rolled oats (gluten-free if needed)

3 tbsp (30 g) milled flaxseed

½ tbsp (3 g) smoked paprika

½ tsp dried oregano

Pinch salt

Freshly ground black pepper

1 tbsp (15 ml) extra-virgin olive oil

**To make the "meatballs": Preheat the oven to 400°F/200°C (180°C convection) and line a baking sheet with parchment paper.**

Roughly chop the onion and garlic and tip them in the food processor along with the tomato puree, lemon zest, soy sauce and balsamic vinegar. Pulse until the onions are in smaller pieces. Then add the drained black beans, oats, milled flaxseed, smoked paprika, dried oregano and a good pinch of salt and pepper. Blitz again until the ingredients bind into a rough paste. Now using a tablespoon as a rough size guide, scoop out the mix and with lightly wet hands, roll into small balls.

In a large skillet, heat the olive oil and gently add the balls, turning them occasionally for 6 to 8 minutes, until they turn light brown all over the outside. Remove the balls from the skillet and spread them out on the lined baking sheet. Place in the oven and bake for 25 minutes.

(continued)

# Tasty Meat-Free Balls with Spaghetti (Continued)

1 tbsp (15 ml) extra-virgin olive oil

2 cloves garlic, crushed

1 tbsp (16 g) tomato puree

1 (14-oz [400-g]) can passata

½ tsp dried oregano

Pinch salt

Freshly ground black pepper

1 tbsp (15 ml) balsamic vinegar

1 tbsp (15 ml) grade A maple syrup

PASTA

Dried spaghetti (2–3 oz [56 to 84 g] per person; gluten-free if needed)

Fresh basil leaves

**To make the tomato sauce:** Heat the olive oil in a pan over medium heat and add the garlic. Stir until the garlic is lightly golden. Add the tomato puree and stir before pouring in the passata. Bring to a gentle simmer for 10 minutes. Then add the dried oregano, salt, pepper, balsamic vinegar and maple syrup. Stir well to combine.

**To make the pasta:** Bring a large saucepan to boil and cook the spaghetti according to the package instructions; reserve a little of the cooking water, then drain. Return the spaghetti to the pan and stir in the pasta sauce, pouring in a little of the cooking water if needed.

Serve the spaghetti in bowls, adding the balls and some fresh basil leaves.

The balls, pasta and sauce will store in a container in the fridge for up to 2 days. If you are making the balls to freeze, allow them to cool completely, portion into airtight containers and freeze.

# Butter Bean and Mushroom Bake

The perfect, uncomplicated meal to suit those cooler months, this creamy and comforting dish combines butter beans with mushrooms, red bell peppers and kale in a hearty bake topped with herby golden crumbs. We don't really know what else to say other than it's a lovely, stand-alone dish that everyone enjoys.

SERVES: 4    PREP TIME: 15 minutes    COOK TIME: 40 minutes

Preheat the oven to 400°F/200°C (180°C convection).

To make the butter beans and mushrooms: Heat the olive oil in a large skillet over medium heat. Add the leek and cook for 3 minutes, then add the garlic and bell peppers and cook for 4 minutes, until they begin to soften. Tip in the sliced mushrooms, stir and cook for 8 minutes.

Add the drained butter beans, chopped kale and smoked paprika. Stir. Pour in the crème fraîche and add the mustard powder, fresh thyme and nutritional yeast. Crumble in the stock cube, pour over the boiling water and season with salt and pepper. Stir and let simmer for a further 5 minutes. Spoon the butterbean and mushroom bake into a 10 x 7-inch (27 x 18-cm) ovenproof dish.

To make the herb crumb topping: Mix together the bread crumbs, thyme, seeds, nutritional yeast, salt and pepper. Sprinkle over the bake and place in the oven for 20 minutes, until the top is golden and the bake is bubbling.

To store, allow to cool completely and then store in an airtight container in the fridge for up to 2 days or freeze in portion sizes.

## BUTTER BEANS AND MUSHROOMS

1–2 tbsp (15–30 ml) extra-virgin olive oil

1 medium leek, finely diced

2 cloves garlic, grated

2 red bell peppers, finely sliced

12 oz (350 g) mushrooms, sliced

1 (13.5-oz [380-g]) can butter beans, drained

5 oz (150 g) kale

1 tsp smoked paprika

7 oz (200 g) vegan crème fraîche

1 tsp mustard powder

2 sprigs of fresh thyme, leaves only (or 1 tsp dried thyme)

1 tbsp (5 g) nutritional yeast

1 vegetable stock cube

½ cup (110 ml) boiling water

Pinch salt

Freshly ground black pepper

## HERB CRUMB

1½ cups (162 g) bread crumbs (gluten-free if needed)

2 sprigs fresh thyme

2 tbsp (18 g) mixed seeds (pumpkin, sunflower)

1 tbsp nutritional yeast

Pinch salt

Freshly ground black pepper

# Ramen Noodle Bowl

Our children have always loved noodle bowls, and a ramen bowl is their favorite. They are easy to make, it's easy to change the ingredients to suit the seasons and they are quick and incredibly satisfying. As the children's taste buds have developed, we have varied the broth's depth of flavor by tweaking the ingredients. Some like it spicy and others like the comfort of a light warming broth. The key ingredient to the ramen broth is miso, a traditional Japanese seasoning made from fermented soy beans. This creates the ultra-savory "umami" flavor that cuts through with zingy and satisfying warmth. Miso comes in a variety of colors and each one has a slightly different flavor. We like this dish best with mild white miso, but encourage you to try it with other types of miso if you like.

**SERVES:** 4     **PREP TIME:** 10 to 15 minutes     **COOK TIME:** 30 minutes

1½ quarts (1½ L) vegetable stock

½ oz (15 g) dried mushrooms (shitake, wild or porcini)

1-inch (2½-cm) piece fresh ginger, thickly sliced

3 cloves garlic, crushed

1 lemongrass stem, sliced

½ tsp coriander seeds

1 cinnamon stick

3 spring onions, white and green stem separated, divided

3 carrots, sliced into long ribbons with a potato peeler

7 oz (200 g) rice noodles

12 (300 g) brown mushrooms, sliced

2 tbsp (32 g) miso paste

1 tbsp (15 ml) mirin or rice vinegar

2 tbsp (30 ml) soy sauce or tamari

Juice of 1 lime

1 tbsp (15 ml) grade A maple syrup

Pinch salt

Freshly ground black pepper

3 cups (100 g) baby spinach

**TO SERVE**

¼ cup (4 g) fresh cilantro leaves

10 radishes, sliced

¼ cup (23 g) fresh mint leaves

1 lime, cut into wedges

6 ears of baby corn

Fresh red chili slices (optional)

Bring the vegetable stock to a boil in a medium saucepan. Then add the dried mushrooms, ginger, garlic, lemongrass, coriander seeds, cinnamon stick and the white spring onions. Reduce the heat to a low simmer and cook for 20 minutes.

Meanwhile, put the carrots and the rice noodles into a heatproof bowl and cover with boiling water. Leave to soften for 10 minutes.

Pour the broth through a strainer and into a second pan and place over medium to high heat. Bring back to a boil, add the mushrooms, then reduce the heat and simmer for 5 minutes. Stir in the miso paste, mirin, soy sauce, lime juice and maple syrup, then add a small pinch of salt and a good grind of black pepper. Drop the spinach into the broth and let it wilt, then use a slotted spoon to lift it out, along with the mushrooms, and divide them among four bowls.

Drain the noodles and carrots and divide them among the bowls. Ladle over the broth. Finish by garnishing with the green spring onions, cilantro, radishes, mint leaves, wedges of lime, baby corn and chili slices, if using.

# Zucchini and Pea Carbonara

This quick pasta dish is perfect for a mid-week meal. It is light and creamy with a touch of fresh zesty lemon, pan-fried zucchini and peas—simply delicious. You will notice that there are several pasta-based dishes in this book; this is because they are always a hit with our kids and their friends. When the children pile in after school, we like to rustle up this dish as we know there will be clean bowls and filled tummies at the end of the meal.

SERVES: 4     PREP TIME: 10 minutes     COOK TIME: 15 minutes

Bring a large saucepan of water to a boil and cook the pasta according to the package instructions.

Tip the frozen peas into a large bowl and pour over enough boiling water to cover them. Leave to stand for 3 minutes, then drain and return the peas to the bowl.

Add the oil to a large skillet and heat over medium to high heat, then add the shallots and garlic. Cook for 3 to 4 minutes, until the shallots start to soften, then add the zucchini ribbons. Stir, then add most of the parsley (reserving a few leaves for serving). Reduce the heat.

In the bowl with the peas, add the cream, nutritional yeast, mustard powder, lemon zest, a good grind of black pepper and a good pinch of salt. Whisk the sauce together, then pour over the vegetables in the skillet.

Once the pasta is cooked, drain and add the pasta to the pan with the vegetables. Toss the pasta with the vegetables and sauce until everything is hot and coated.

Serve immediately, sharing the pasta between bowls. Sprinkle over a few fresh parsley leaves, a grind of black pepper and dried chili flakes if desired.

NOTE: *This sauce works well with any kind of pasta shape.*

*Dried tagliatelle pasta (about 2–3 oz [50–75 g] per person) (gluten-free if needed)*

*1⅓ cups (200 g) frozen peas*

*1 tbsp (15 ml) extra-virgin olive oil*

*2 shallots, finely sliced*

*2 cloves garlic, finely sliced*

*2 zucchini, sliced into long ribbons with a potato peeler*

*Handful fresh parsley, roughly chopped, divided*

*1¼ cups (300 ml) vegan cream*

*3 tbsp (15 g) nutritional yeast*

*1 tsp mustard powder*

*Zest of ½ lemon*

*Freshly ground black pepper*

*Pinch salt*

OPTIONAL ADDITIONS
*Dried chili flakes*

# Sweet Chili and Ginger Tofu with Vegetable Rice

From the time they were tiny, our children have loved anything that is "sweet chili"-flavored (not hot chili). They enjoy the sticky, slightly sweet taste with salty soy sauce that adds that depth of flavor. Clearly, this being the case, we have used it to our parental advantage and created this dish packed with plant-based protein and filled with vegetables. We use organic tofu as it is brilliant at absorbing flavor and being coated in sauce. We've added extra vegetables into the rice. These can be from any frozen mixed vegetable bags you have or diced veg from the fridge; even tinned corn and peas will give a boost.

SERVES/MAKES: 4    PREP TIME: 15 minutes    COOK TIME: 25 minutes

## RICE

1 cup (200 g) brown rice

2 tbsp (30 ml) extra-virgin olive oil

2 to 3 cups (weight varies) mixed vegetables (either a frozen mix, or a mix cut into small pieces; e.g., red bell pepper, spring onions, peas, corn, broccoli, edamame beans, spinach)

1 tbsp (15 ml) soy sauce or tamari

2 tbsp (30 ml) water (optional)

## TOFU

17 oz (480 g) organic firm tofu

2–4 tbsp (30–60 g) cornstarch (use up to 4 tbsp to make the sauce thicker)

1–2 tbsp (15–30 ml) extra-virgin olive oil

## SWEET CHILI–GINGER SAUCE

6 tbsp (90 ml) soy sauce or tamari

2 tbsp (30 ml) apple cider vinegar

2 tbsp (30 ml) grade A maple syrup

2 tbsp (30 g) tomato puree

Juice of 1 lime

1-inch (2.5-cm) piece of fresh ginger, grated

1 tsp garlic powder

½–1 tsp dried chili flakes

Pinch salt

Freshly ground black pepper

**To start the rice:** Cook the rice according to the package instructions.

**To prepare the tofu:** Drain it first and use some kitchen paper towels to remove any excess liquid. Then cut the tofu into cubes, roughly 1-inch (2-cm) squares.

**To make the sauce:** In a large bowl, whisk together the soy sauce, apple cider vinegar, maple syrup, tomato puree and lime juice. Grate in the ginger and add the garlic powder, chili flakes, salt and pepper, then whisk.

Transfer the cubed tofu into the sauce, stir carefully so that it is all coated and leave for 10 to 15 minutes. Then sprinkle over the cornstarch and stir to coat all the pieces.

**To cook the tofu:** Heat the olive oil in a large skillet over medium to high heat and add the tofu, leaving the remaining sauce in the bowl. Cook the tofu for 8 to 10 minutes, until all sides are golden. Pour in the remaining sauce and stir until the tofu is coated in a sticky glaze.

**To cook the vegetable rice:** Heat another skillet over medium heat. Pour in the 2 tablespoons (30 ml) of olive oil, then add all the chopped vegetables (except the spinach leaves, if using) and stir-fry, stirring frequently, for 4 to 5 minutes until golden. Then add the cooked rice and stir in. Pour over the soy sauce and add the spinach, if using. Stir for a couple of minutes until the spinach has wilted. To prevent the rice from sticking, add a couple of tablespoons of water, if needed.

Serve the sweet chili and ginger tofu with the vegetable rice.

# Asparagus, Potato and Pea Open Tart

We admit it, we've cheated. Well, it's not cheating, it's using our time wisely. We use store-bought puff pastry to make the base of this tart, making it quick to create. The crisp puff pastry is layered with a creamy butter bean hummus and topped with tender asparagus, sliced new potatoes, peas, fresh mint and toasted pine nuts. It looks impressive, but remains easy to make. Perfect for a light dinner with a potato salad and lots of fresh salad leaves. We always have some ready-made pastry on hand in the freezer for making this dish. The children call this our "posh pizza."

SERVES: 4 to 6    PREP TIME: 20 minutes    COOK TIME: 20 minutes

Preheat the oven to 400°F/200°C (180°C convection).

Line a large baking sheet with parchment paper and mix together the unsweetened plant-based milk and Worcestershire sauce in a small bowl.

Unroll the puff pastry onto the large baking sheet. Use a small sharp knife to score a 1-inch (2-cm)-wide border around the pastry and prick the base lightly all over with a fork. Brush the border with the plant-based milk and Worcestershire sauce glaze. Place in the oven and bake for 15 minutes until golden and cooked.

Meanwhile, bring a large saucepan of water to a boil, and cook the new potatoes for 8 to 10 minutes or until tender. Drain and allow the potatoes to cool slightly before slicing thinly. Parboil the asparagus for 3 minutes, adding the peas for the last minute. Drain and set aside.

To make the butter bean hummus, put the drained butter beans in a food processor along with the grated garlic, lemon zest and juice, olive oil, light tahini, salt and pepper. Then, blend to make a smooth puree.

Spoon the hummus into the center of the pastry and smooth it across the base. Top with the sliced potatoes, asparagus, peas, crumbled vegan feta, pine nuts and some roughly shredded fresh mint. Slice and serve.

Cover and store any leftovers in the fridge overnight.

NOTE: *The butter bean hummus is one of our favorite hummus recipes and there's always a pot in the fridge. The hummus will keep for 4 days in the fridge in an airtight container.*

2 tbsp (30 ml) unsweetened plant-based milk

1 tsp vegan Worcestershire sauce

10 oz (280 g) chilled ready-rolled vegan puff pastry sheet (gluten-free if needed)

9 oz (250 g) small new potatoes, cooked and thinly sliced

7 oz (200 g) asparagus

½ cup (65 g) peas (fresh or frozen)

1 (13.5-oz [380-g]) can butter beans, drained

1 clove garlic, grated

Zest and juice of 1 lemon

3 tbsp (45 ml) extra-virgin olive oil

1 tbsp (15 ml) light tahini

Pinch salt

Freshly ground black pepper

2 oz (50 g) vegan feta

2 tbsp (20 g) toasted pine nuts

Small handful fresh mint leaves

# Squash Satay and Dippers

This is a tasty twist on peanut satay sauce. Here we've added roasted butternut squash to give a caramelized sweetness with the added bonus of including another vegetable.

This scrumptious squash satay is hard to resist and we all happily eat it with a spoon straight from the pot. It's one of our go-to secret weapon recipes for when we want to get our children to eat a rainbow of vegetables without them complaining.

It is easy to make and incredibly versatile—it works well whether served hot, warm, cold, dunked, drizzled or stirred into other dishes. Here we share how to use the sauce to roast a stack of gorgeous veg and lots of ideas as to what can be dunked in it—from sweet potato wedges to zucchini batons.

Don't be daunted by the cook time, most of it is hands-off roasting in the oven. The satay takes about 45 minutes to make; an additional 30 minutes is required to roast the satay-covered vegetables. Save time by roasting the squash the day before.

---

**SERVES:** 4    **PREP TIME:** 15 minutes    **COOK TIME:** 1 hour 15 minutes

---

**SQUASH SATAY SAUCE**

*1 medium butternut squash*

*Extra-virgin olive oil*

*Large pinch salt*

*Freshly ground black pepper*

*1 (13.5-oz [400 ml]) can coconut milk*

*2 tbsp (30 g) peanut butter (almond butter also works)*

*1 clove garlic*

*1½-inch (4-cm) piece fresh ginger*

*2 tbsp (30 ml) soy sauce or tamari*

*1 tsp medium curry powder*

*Juice of ½ lime*

To make the squash satay sauce: Preheat the oven to 400°F/200°C (180°C convection). Line 1 medium and 1 large baking sheet with parchment paper.

Peel the butternut squash, slice into ½-inch (1-cm)-thick pieces and remove the seeds. Then cut into cubes. Spread the squash cubes out on the medium lined baking sheet and drizzle with oil. Sprinkle with salt and black pepper. Place in the oven and cook for 40 minutes.

(continued)

# Squash Satay and Dippers (Continued)

## ROASTED VEGETABLES
*2 bell peppers, quartered*

*7 oz (200 g) mushrooms, halved*

*7 oz (200 g) broccoli florets*

*3 medium carrots*

## RAW VEGETABLES FOR DIPPING
*Baby corn*

*Sugar snap peas*

*Carrot batons*

*Cucumber sticks*

*Tomatoes*

*Zucchini batons*

**To make the roasted vegetables:** Meanwhile, roughly slice the bell peppers, mushrooms, broccoli and carrots, and spread them out onto the large baking sheet. Set aside.

After 40 minutes, remove the roasted squash from the oven and tip half the squash pieces into a heatproof blender or a food processor. Now pour in the can of coconut milk, add the peanut butter, grate in the garlic and ginger, and add the soy sauce, curry powder and lime juice. Blend until smooth.

Drizzle half the squash satay sauce lightly over the vegetables on the large baking sheet, and place it in the oven. Roast for 30 minutes.

Transfer the remaining squash satay sauce to a bowl. Prepare the raw vegetables.

To serve, place all the roasted vegetables on large platters in the middle of the table and let everyone choose. We find that smaller children like to have their own pots of the satay. Store any remaining sauce in a jar in the fridge for up to 5 days.

NOTE: *You can either make a second batch of the satay sauce with the remaining roasted squash or drizzle it with the satay sauce and place in the oven to heat through for 10 minutes and eat.*

# Beet and Mint Falafels

Falafels are brilliant, a seriously tasty and healthy plant-based fast food. We'd always put off making our own falafels, believing them to be complicated—more fool us, as they aren't! Falafels are easy—our simple recipe uses a chickpea base (butter beans and broad beans will work as well), and for ease, mixes in precooked beets with fresh mint and a zingy squeeze of lemon juice. Enjoy them in a wrap with our cool tahini dressing, serve with a big salad or eat them on their own, dunked into a tasty dip.

We like to make a double batch as the falafels travel well, making them a great addition to lunch boxes and picnics.

MAKES: 18 falafels and 6 flatbreads    PREP TIME: 20 minutes + 1 hour to proof the flatbreads
COOK TIME: 25 minutes

**To make the flatbreads:** Tip the flour into a large mixing bowl, add the salt and sugar to one side and the dried yeast to the other. Make a well in the center of the flour, pour in the olive oil and gradually pour in the water, bringing the ingredients together with a wooden spoon. Then bring the dough together using your hands. Tip it onto a lightly floured surface and knead for 5 minutes until the dough is smooth.

Lightly oil the sides of the mixing bowl and place the dough in it. Cover with a clean tea towel and leave to rise for an hour. If needed, this dough can be stored, covered in the fridge, for up to 24 hours.

Lightly flour a surface and tip the dough onto it. Fold and knead it, knocking the air out. Divide the dough into six equal pieces. Roll each piece of dough into a ball and use a rolling pin to roll each ball into a circle about 8 inches (20 cm) in diameter.

Heat a large skillet over high heat and add a little olive oil. Swirl it around the pan then add the first flatbread. Cook for 2 to 3 minutes, then flip it over and cook the other side for a couple more minutes. Repeat with the rest of the dough.

**To prepare the tahini dressing:** Place the tahini, yogurt, lemon juice and maple syrup into a bowl and stir together until you have a smooth dressing. Set aside until ready to serve.

**To prepare the red onion and lime pickle:** Place the finely sliced onion into a bowl, squeeze over the lime juice, stir and set aside for 20 minutes while you make the falafels.

(continued)

## FLATBREADS
1¾ cups plus 1 tbsp (250 g) bread flour

1 tsp salt

1 tbsp (15 g) superfine caster sugar

1½ tsp (5 g) dried instant yeast

1 tbsp (15 ml) extra-virgin olive oil, plus extra for greasing the bowl and cooking the breads

⅔ cup (160 ml) water

## TAHINI AND YOGURT DRESSING
2 tbsp (30 ml) light tahini

½ cup (60 ml) unsweetened vegan coconut yogurt

Juice of ½ lemon

1 tsp grade A maple syrup

## RED ONION AND LIME PICKLE
1 red onion, finely sliced

Juice of 1 lime

# Beet and Mint Falafels (Continued)

To make the beet and mint falafels: Preheat the oven to 400°F/200°C (180°C convection) and line a medium baking sheet with parchment paper. Add ½ tablespoon (7 ml) of olive oil to a small skillet over medium heat, tip in the onion and cook for 5 minutes, until soft, stirring frequently. Then add the cumin, coriander and garlic and cook for a further 2 minutes.

Transfer the onion mixture carefully into a food processor. Then add the drained chickpeas, chopped beets, mint leaves, tahini, gram flour, salt, pepper and lemon juice. Pulse the ingredients until they combine and form a rough paste.

Tip the falafel mix into a bowl and, with damp hands or 2 spoons, shape the mixture into 18 falafels. You can make them into round balls or use spoons to create more of a kernel shape.

Add the remaining 1½ tablespoons (22 ml) of olive oil to a large skillet and place over medium heat. Pan-fry the falafels for 2 to 3 minutes on each side, until golden brown. Then transfer them to the baking sheet and bake for 20 minutes.

To assemble: Place a few mixed leaves in the center of a flatbread, add some falafels, sliced radish, pickled red onion and a drizzle of tahini dressing. Repeat with the other flatbreads.

Store any leftover falafels, dressing and quick pickle in separate airtight containers in the fridge for up to 2 days. To store the flatbreads, cover them in parchment paper and roll up; eat within 24 hours.

## FALAFELS

2 tbsp (30 ml) extra-virgin olive oil, divided, plus more for pan-frying

1 small red onion, finely chopped

1 tsp ground cumin

½ tsp ground coriander

1 clove garlic, crushed

1 (13-oz [370-g]) can chickpeas, drained

6 oz (180 g) precooked beets, roughly chopped

20 fresh mint leaves

1 tbsp (15 ml) light tahini

½ cup (60 g) gram flour (chickpea flour)

¼ tsp salt

Freshly ground black pepper

Juice of ½ lemon

## TO SERVE

Mixed salad leaves

Radishes, sliced

# Batch Cooking and Freezer Meals

If there's ever a set of recipes to make our lives easier, it is this delicious collection. We can't cook from scratch every night, and these recipes will save you time, money and energy, as well as help you to reduce food waste. This is where batch cooking, planning ahead and using your freezer comes in handy—it's a lifesaver for a busy family life when you do not want to rely on overprocessed, packaged ready meals. All that is required is for you to defrost the meal, perhaps cook some rice and add a scattering of fresh herbs or your favorite side dish.

Our freezers are full of portioned meals for days when we can't all eat together, such as when after-school activities take over or one of us has to work late. Try to label the containers—we admit that we do sometimes forget, and this can make mealtimes all the more interesting. We often double the quantities of a recipe when batch cooking, so we eat half right away and freeze the other half. Batch cooking is so easy to do, making enough to eat for lunch, a meal another day or to freeze, which means you always have nutritious delicious meals ready to go.

Often while making Sunday dinner, we will cook a couple of recipes from this chapter. This way we don't lose precious time on the weekend, but we gain helpful hours during the week. We particularly love meals that can be cooked in one pot and get great pleasure from seeing and smelling a simmering pot of delicious food with tantalizing aromas filling the kitchen. Simply chop, stir and occasionally check the pot to see how it's getting along.

These recipes were created to be incredibly flexible. Make a large pot of the Three-Bean Chili (page 85) and serve with rice one day, in a baked potato another, wrapped up in a burrito or loaded on top of nachos with vegan melted cheese, salsa and guacamole. It's perfect for a Friday night when we've had quite enough of feeding everyone and need a quick and tasty dinner solution. The Lentil, Coconut and Spinach Dahl (page 90) is another recipe that can be served in different ways—cooking with lentils adds important fiber to the meal, as well as creating a seriously creamy dish with warming spices. Enjoy it scooped into large bowls with rice, chapatis or a spoonful of yogurt and fresh cilantro. This really is food for the soul.

You will find many other recipes in the book that are also great for batch cooking and freezing. Check out the Creamy Vegetable Curry (page 112), Tasty Meat-Free Balls with Spaghetti (page 61) and the Tomato, Pepper and Cannellini Bean Pasta Bake (page 104). One of the other speedy cheats we use is to freeze the Green Pesto (page 45) and the Thai Green Curry paste (page 120) in ice cube trays. Once frozen, tip them into freezer bags or boxes, ready to bring out to turn into dinner. Both pastes are a handy way to make sure spinach and fresh herbs never go to waste.

# Cottage Pie with Cauliflower and Potato Mash

This is a tasty twist on the classic cottage pie, a reassuringly familiar and hearty meal topped with a delicious blend of cauliflower and potato mash; it is cozy comfort food at its best. We have used more traditional vegetables in the base, but the key is to include the cannellini beans as they are brilliantly filling, high in fiber, and they add a mild, slightly nutty flavor. You can serve this dish on its own, though we enjoy it with roasted vegetables. The children love a large dollop of brown sauce or tomato ketchup on the side.

SERVES: 4    PREP TIME: 20 minutes    COOK TIME: 1 hour

**To make the topping:** Preheat the oven to 400°F/200°C (180°C convection) and line a medium baking sheet with parchment paper.

Remove the cauliflower florets from the main stem and cauliflower leaves. Roughly slice the stem. Spread the cauliflower out on the baking sheet, drizzle with 2 tablespoons (30 ml) of extra-virgin olive oil and rub it over the florets and stem. Place in the middle of the oven and cook for 30 minutes.

Meanwhile, peel and slice the potatoes into chunks, place in a saucepan, cover with water and boil until the potatoes are soft enough to insert a fork (this takes about 10 minutes). Drain and set to one side.

(continued)

## TOPPING

*1 small cauliflower*

*4 tbsp (60 ml) extra-virgin olive oil, divided*

*1 lb 5 oz (600 g) potatoes*

*⅓ cup (80 ml) unsweetened plant-based milk*

*2 tbsp (10 g) nutritional yeast*

*Pinch salt*

*Freshly ground black pepper*

**To make the base:** Add the olive oil to a large saucepan over low to medium heat. Next add the onion, celery and carrot and cook for 5 minutes, until the onion and celery start to soften. Add the tomato puree and stir. Tip in the cannellini beans, mushrooms and bell pepper to the saucepan and cook until the mushrooms start to soften.

Now add the Worcestershire sauce, frozen peas, salt and pepper. Crumble in the stock cube, then pour over the boiling water. Stir and gently simmer for 20 minutes. Then, using a potato masher, lightly crush the filling.

Remove the cauliflower from the oven. Tip the potatoes and cauliflower back into the pan the potatoes were cooked in. Pour in the unsweetened plant-based milk, 2 tablespoons (30 ml) of extra-virgin olive oil and the nutritional yeast, and season with a little salt and pepper. Use the potato masher to mash the potatoes and cauliflower together.

Spoon the cottage pie filling into a 10 x 7-inch (27 cm x 18-cm) oven dish. Top with spoonfuls of the cauliflower mash mixture and run a fork over the mash to rough the top.

Place on a baking sheet into the center of the oven and cook for 30 minutes, until the filling is bubbling and the top is golden and crunchy in places. Serve straight from the oven.

To freeze, allow the cottage pie to cool completely, divide into portions and freeze in lidded freezer-proof containers. Alternatively, make the cottage pie base mixture and the mashed potato and cauliflower topping, then freeze the two separately. To reheat, leave in the fridge overnight to defrost thoroughly. Then place the base in an ovenproof dish, cover with the mash and heat in the oven for 25 minutes, until hot in the middle.

BASE

1 tbsp (15 ml) extra-virgin olive oil

1 white onion, finely diced

1 stick of celery, diced

1 medium carrot, diced

1 tbsp (16 g) tomato puree

1 (14-oz [400-g]) can cannellini beans, drained

7 oz (200 g) mushrooms, roughly chopped

1 red bell pepper, roughly chopped

1 tbsp (15 ml) vegan Worcestershire sauce

1 cup (145 g) frozen peas

Pinch salt

Freshly ground black pepper

1 vegetable stock cube

1¼ cups (300 ml) boiling water

# Three-Bean Chili

If someone asked us which of our core recipes is the one we make repeatedly, is unbelievably satisfying, freezer-friendly, asked for the most, a time-saver and incredibly versatile, then this Three-Bean Chili recipe would definitely be top of the list. Ladle into a large bowl and eat on its own or with rice, fresh cilantro and a spoonful of yogurt; spoon it on a baked potato; layer into nachos with salsa and grated vegan cheese; or fold into a wrap with guacamole—the possibilities are endless! Maybe that's why we love it so much. Don't be overwhelmed by the number of ingredients. There's minimal chopping, then everything goes into one deep pot and cooks slowly with only an occasional stir. Because it is full of healthy proteins and packed full of flavor, this recipe is one you will want to double-batch to freeze for another day. Then there is always a nutritious and delicious meal on hand.

SERVES: 6    PREP TIME: 10 minutes    COOK TIME: 45 minutes to 1 hour 15 minutes

*1 tbsp (15 ml) extra-virgin olive oil*

*1 red onion, finely diced or chopped*

*1 celery stalk, diced*

*1 red bell pepper, diced*

*2 cloves garlic, finely diced*

*2 tbsp (32 g) tomato puree*

*1 tsp ground cinnamon*

*1 tsp ground cumin*

*1 tsp ground coriander*

*1 tsp smoked paprika*

*½ tsp chili powder*

*1 (14-oz [400-g]) can kidney beans, drained*

*1 (14-oz [400-g]) can chickpeas, drained*

*1 (14-oz [400-g]) can black beans, drained*

*2 (14-oz [400-g]) cans chopped tomatoes*

*1 vegetable stock cube*

*⅔ cup (150 ml) water*

*1 tbsp (15 ml) balsamic vinegar*

*1 tbsp (15 ml) grade A maple syrup*

*1 tsp vegan Worcestershire sauce*

*Pinch salt*

*½ tsp freshly ground black pepper*

Place the olive oil into a large deep saucepan and bring to medium heat. Add the onion and celery and cook for 3 minutes before adding the bell pepper and garlic. Stir and cook for a further 8 minutes, until the vegetables have softened and started to caramelize.

Add the tomato puree and the spices: cinnamon, cumin, coriander, smoked paprika and chili powder. Stir them into the vegetables until the spices release a strong aroma, about 30 seconds.

Now tip in the kidney beans, chickpeas and black beans. Pour over the canned tomatoes and stir. Crumble in the stock cube and pour in the water; stir and bring the chili to a boil. Add the balsamic vinegar, maple syrup, vegan Worcestershire sauce, salt and pepper and stir through.

**(continued)**

# Three-Bean Chili (Continued)

SERVING SUGGESTIONS

*Cooked brown rice, baked potatoes or wraps*

*Guacamole and/or sliced or chopped avocado*

*Fresh cilantro*

*Fresh chili slices*

*Unsweetened vegan coconut yogurt*

Reduce the heat to a gentle simmer and cover the pan with a lid, leaving the stirring spoon in to create a small gap for the steam to escape. Cook for 45 minutes, stirring occasionally to stop it from scorching on the bottom of the pan. The chili could be served now, but ideally, we like to cook the chili for another 30 minutes on low heat.

Serve with rice, over a baked potato, in a wrap or in a bowl with guacamole and any other toppings you'd like.

Once the chili is fully cooled, portion it into airtight containers and store in the fridge for up to 3 days or freeze. Defrost thoroughly before reheating.

# Mushroom Stroganoff

This easy vegan twist on the classic creamy Stroganoff takes under 30 minutes to be on the table and also reheats well, making it ideal for a quick weeknight dinner. Full of smoky and umami flavors, this recipe is a satisfying dish that you will make time and time again.

For ease, feel free to use whatever mushrooms are readily available, but we highly recommend, if you can, including seasonal mushroom varieties. These can really elevate the dish, adding more layers of flavor. If your children are small, maybe start making this dish with white mushrooms (as they have a milder flavor), then gradually mix the mushroom types as their taste buds develop. We like to use a vegan crème fraîche for this recipe and tend to use one that's made from oats. If a similar product is not available, unsweetened vegan heavy cream works equally well.

SERVES: 4    PREP TIME: 10 minutes    COOK TIME: 20 minutes

In a large, flat-bottomed saucepan or skillet, heat the olive oil over medium heat. Add the onion and garlic and cook for a couple of minutes before adding all the mushrooms. Cook for 10 minutes, stirring frequently, until the mushrooms have started to soften.

Now add the paprika and stir into the mushrooms before adding the vegan crème fraîche, Dijon mustard, nutritional yeast, Worcestershire sauce, salt and pepper.

Allow the mushrooms to slowly simmer for about 10 minutes until the sauce has reduced a little. Then stir in the fresh parsley just before serving. Serve with wild rice.

Place in an airtight container in the fridge for up to 2 days or in the freezer. Defrost thoroughly before reheating in a saucepan.

1 tbsp (15 ml) extra-virgin olive oil

1 red onion, finely sliced

2 cloves garlic, crushed and sliced

1 lb 9 oz (700 g) mixed mushrooms, sliced (large flat mushrooms, brown mushrooms, white or seasonal varieties)

1½ tsp (3 g) smoked paprika

½ cup (125 ml) vegan crème fraîche

½–1½ tsp Dijon mustard (use ½ tsp for younger children)

2 tbsp (10 g) nutritional yeast

1 tbsp (15 ml) vegan Worcestershire sauce

Pinch salt

Freshly ground black pepper

Good handful fresh parsley, roughly chopped

TO SERVE
Cooked mixed wild rice

# Lentil, Coconut and Spinach Dahl

During the cooler months we make a large batch of dahl at least twice a month. Dahl is filled with nourishing, inexpensive and readily available ingredients and has to be one of the most uncomplicated recipes to make. Like our Three-Bean Chili (page 85), it is a dish we crave if we've not eaten it for a while. Watching the whole family sit down and soak up the scent of the warming spices, dip in a chapati or scoop up a mouthful with vegan yogurt and rice makes us very satisfied cooks.

SERVES: 4 to 6      PREP TIME: 10 minutes      COOK TIME: 40 minutes to 1 hour

1 tbsp (15 ml) extra-virgin olive oil

1 red onion, finely diced

2 cloves garlic, crushed

Thumb-size piece fresh ginger (20 g), grated

1 small fresh red chili

1 tbsp (16 g) tomato puree

1 tsp ground cumin

½ tsp ground coriander

1 tsp mustard seeds

½ tsp ground turmeric

1 tbsp (6 g) garam masala

1⅓ cups (250 g) dried split red lentils

1 (14-oz [400-g]) can chopped tomatoes

1 (13.5-oz [380-ml]) can coconut milk

1 cup (150 g) fresh cherry tomatoes, halved

1 vegetable stock cube

1 cup (240 ml) boiling water

3⅓ cups (100 g) fresh spinach leaves

1 cup (15 g) fresh cilantro, roughly chopped

Juice of ½ lemon

Pinch salt

Freshly ground black pepper

**TO SERVE**

Fresh cilantro leaves

Fresh chili slices

Fresh sliced tomatoes

Unsweetened vegan coconut yogurt

Naan bread or chapatis

Brown rice

Pour the oil into a large, deep saucepan over medium heat. Add the onion and cook, stirring occasionally, for 5 minutes until it starts to soften. Add the garlic, grated ginger, fresh chili and tomato puree and stir for 3 to 4 minutes before adding the cumin, coriander, mustard seeds, turmeric and garam masala. Allow the spices to cook through for a few minutes, until everything in the pan is soft and fragrant.

Tip in the lentils, chopped tomatoes, coconut milk and cherry tomatoes. Crumble over the vegetable stock cube and pour in the boiling water. Stir thoroughly and bring the dahl to a simmer. Cover the pan with a lid, leaving the stirring spoon in to create a small gap for the steam to escape.

Cook for 30 minutes until the lentils have softened, stirring occasionally. Stir in the spinach leaves, cilantro and lemon juice. Taste the dahl and add more lemon juice, if needed, then season with a pinch of salt and pepper. Stir and cook until the spinach leaves have wilted. Eat straight away or enhance the flavor by cooking over low heat for 25 more minutes.

Spoon the dahl into bowls, top with fresh cilantro leaves, a few slices of chili, slices of tomato and a dollop of coconut yogurt, and serve with your favorite flatbread or rice.

Once the dahl is fully cooled, portion into airtight containers and store in the fridge for up to 2 days or freeze. Defrost thoroughly before reheating.

# Sausage, Chickpea and Smoked Paprika Stew

A hearty and sustaining stew is a must-have recipe for any family cook, especially in the cooler months. We love the simple flavors of the rich tomato and smoky paprika sauce.

We'd also recommend finding a good quality vegan sausage. We prefer sausages that are made with mushrooms, herbs and leeks rather than the soy-based vegan sausages—but use what you can find and what suits your family's taste buds. In this recipe, we have used vegan sausage swirls. Also, if you don't have chickpeas or want to change the recipe a little, we often add cannellini or butter beans instead, as these work beautifully in stews.

SERVES: 4    PREP TIME: 15 minutes    COOK TIME: 40 minutes

Place a large, deep saucepan over medium to high heat and pour in the olive oil. Add the onion, leek, carrots and sausages and cook for 5 minutes. Keep turning the sausages until they are golden brown on the outside and the onion softens.

Add the garlic, chickpeas, smoked paprika, rosemary and oregano and cook for another 4 minutes. Add a small splash of water if the ingredients start to stick to the pan. Add the sun-dried tomato or tomato puree paste and cook for a couple of minutes, stirring everything together.

Next add the canned chopped tomatoes, passata, vegetable stock cube and seasoning. Pour in the boiling water and stir through. Bring to a simmer and add the baby corn and frozen vegetables, stir and cover with the pan lid, leaving the spoon in the pan so the lid sits ajar. Gently simmer for 20 minutes, until the vegetables are tender.

Roughly chop the parsley and add three-quarters of it to the pan, reserving the rest for garnish, and stir into the stew.

To serve, ladle into large bowls and sprinkle with the remaining parsley.

To freeze, allow it to cool then freeze in portion sizes. Defrost fully, then reheat in a saucepan over medium heat.

1 tbsp (15 ml) extra-virgin olive oil

1 medium onion, finely sliced

1 leek, finely sliced

2 carrots, roughly chopped

8 vegan sausages

2 cloves garlic, crushed and diced

1 (14-oz [400-g]) can chickpeas, drained

1 tsp smoked paprika

1 tsp dried rosemary

1 tsp dried oregano

1 tbsp (16 g) sun-dried tomato paste or tomato puree

1 (14-oz [400-g]) can chopped tomatoes

7 oz (200 g) passata

1 vegetable stock cube

⅔ cup (150 ml) boiling water

8 ears of baby corn, sliced in half

1 cup (150 g) mixed frozen vegetables (peas, corn, peppers, beans, etc.)

Small handful parsley, divided

Small pinch salt

Freshly ground black pepper

### TO SERVE
Slices of thick crusty sourdough bread, mashed potato, rice or a flatbread

# Moroccan-Inspired Tagine

Tagine is Morocco's best-known dish. Our vegan tagine is filled with chunky vegetables that absorb the essence of all the beautiful spices that are at the heart of this dish. This veggie version is particularly popular with the children—thanks to the dried apricots and the sweet potato, creating a warming sweetness to each mouthful.

The dish on its own is stunning, but we feel the perfect accompaniment is to serve it with fresh mint leaves, pomegranate seeds and quinoa, topped with toasted flaked almonds.

SERVES: 4     PREP TIME: 10 minutes     COOK TIME: 40 minutes

1 tbsp (15 ml) extra-virgin olive oil

1 onion, finely chopped

2 cloves garlic, finely chopped

1 tsp ground cumin

1 tsp ground cinnamon

1 tsp ground smoked paprika

½ tsp ground turmeric

2 tbsp (32 g) tomato puree

1 heaped tsp harissa paste

1 medium (300 g) sweet potato, cut into 1-inch (2-cm) cubes

1 red bell pepper, chopped into bite-size pieces

1 yellow bell pepper, chopped into bite-size pieces

1 zucchini, sliced into small chunks

2 (14-oz [400-g]) cans chopped tomatoes

1 (14-oz [400-g]) can chickpeas, drained

4 oz (100 g) dried apricots, roughly chopped

1 vegetable stock cube

1½ cups (300 ml) boiling water

Juice of ½ lemon

Pinch salt

Freshly ground black pepper

TO SERVE

Cooked quinoa

Toasted flaked almonds

Handful fresh mint or parsley

Pomegranate seeds

Heat the olive oil in a large deep saucepan over medium heat. Add the onion and cook for 5 minutes until it starts to soften, stirring regularly.

Now add the garlic, cumin, cinnamon, smoked paprika, turmeric, tomato puree and harissa paste and cook with the onion for a couple of minutes, until you can smell the aroma of the spices. Then add the chopped sweet potato, bell peppers and zucchini and stir. Next tip in the canned tomatoes, chickpeas and chopped apricots. Crumble over the stock cube, pour in the boiling water and season to taste with lemon juice, salt and pepper. Stir.

Bring to a boil, cover the pan with a lid and reduce the heat to low. Simmer and cook for 25 to 30 minutes, until the vegetables are tender, stirring occasionally.

While the tagine is cooking, cook the quinoa according to the package instructions. Roughly chop the herbs and toast the flaked almonds in a dry skillet for 3 to 4 minutes, until just golden; keep them moving around so they don't burn.

Serve the tagine with quinoa, toasted almond flakes, fresh mint and parsley and a sprinkle of pomegranate seeds.

Once the tagine is fully cooled, portion into airtight containers and store in the fridge for up to 2 days or freeze. Defrost thoroughly before reheating.

# Oven to Table

We love simplicity when it comes to creating our family meals; our favorite recipes are those that make our lives a little easier and embrace taste and texture. In this chapter, you will find a selection of recipes that require minimal prep and the results are beautiful, flavorsome meals. There is something very satisfying about peeling, chopping, stirring, drizzling oil, coating in seasoning, then placing the dish in the oven and waiting for the release of welcoming aromas. One of the greatest joys of these dishes is minimal washing up and the other is that once the dish is in the oven you have time to get on with other things.

These recipes combine layers of flavor including citrus, light spice, fruit and garlic with a variety of wonderful ingredients. As with the mid-week meals, these recipes are an ideal way to introduce new tastes to children. We have used subtle and warming flavors rather than fiery heat or intense spices. A tasty example of this is the Warming Jerk Jackfruit (page 100). With just a hint of spice combined with juicy pineapple, corn on the cob, peppers and sweet potatoes, it's a vibrant feast that balances light spices and sweet flavors.

For those of you who adore a comforting bowl of creamy savory risotto as much as we do, but are put off from making it as it can be time-consuming to cook in the traditional way, you will be as delighted as we are with the Easy Baked Squash Risotto (page 103). Oven-roasting butternut squash until it is sweet and tender and leaving the rice to bake in the oven creates a satisfyingly moreish plate of food. It's simple and utterly delicious.

If you love cauliflower and are struggling to convince your family what a brilliant and versatile vegetable it is, then try the Roasted Golden Vegetables with Lime and Harissa Cauliflower (page 99). The cauliflower florets are coated in vegan coconut yogurt mixed with a hint of spice and roasted. We could quite happily eat cauliflower like this all the time.

Again, we have included recipes to cover the seasons. For those warm summer days, the Warm Summer Salad with Roasted Peaches and Lentils (page 108) is perfect and made tantalizing by a combination of savory lentils with roasted soft sweet peaches, thyme and orange zest. In the winter months, it's hard to beat the Tomato, Pepper and Cannellini Bean Pasta Bake (page 104)—a comforting dish, with a creamy tomato sauce and a golden crust. Serve it straight from the oven and place on the table for everyone to share.

# Roasted Golden Vegetables with Lime and Harissa Cauliflower

We love experimenting with flavors and different ways to cook vegetables to make them more appealing to our children. Many people have a difficult relationship with cauliflower, and it's not a vegetable people often feel excited about. Here we banish the undercooked or overly mushy cauliflower that we grew up with and roast our cauliflower in a sticky vegan coconut yogurt, lime and lightly spiced coating. Once you have tasted cauliflower this way, you may never want to eat it any other. The flavors of the coated cauliflower with chickpeas and roasted vegetables really complement each other. Once the dish is cooked, we serve it liberally drizzled with the yummy light lemon and tahini dressing.

SERVES: 4     PREP TIME: 10 minutes     COOK TIME: 35 minutes

To make the cauliflower: Pre-heat the oven to 425°F/220°C (200°C convection) and line a large baking sheet with parchment paper.

Break the cauliflower into 1-inch (2.5-cm) florets. Spoon the yogurt into a large mixing bowl with the harissa and lime juice and stir together until combined. Then add the cauliflower and stir until the florets are completely covered.

Tip the chickpeas into the base of the prepared tray and spread them out. Nestle the carrots and bell peppers in with the chickpeas and drizzle with olive oil. Then spread the cauliflower out on top.

Place the tray of vegetables in the center of the oven and roast for 20 minutes. Place the clove of garlic on the baking sheet and return to the oven and bake for a further 15 minutes.

To make the tahini dressing: Meanwhile, in a small bowl, combine the coconut yogurt, light tahini, maple syrup and lemon juice. Stir until silky smooth.

Remove the baking sheet from the oven, take the clove of garlic from the tray and set aside to cool slightly. Spread the spinach leaves over the hot roasted vegetables and stir them in until the leaves wilt.

Peel the cooked clove of garlic and, using the back of a spoon, squash it into a smooth paste. Then scrape it up with a knife and stir the paste into the tahini and lemon dressing.

Roughly chop the mint leaves and sprinkle them over the vegetables on the tray. Then generously drizzle over the tahini dressing and serve with a leafy green salad.

## CAULIFLOWER

*1 medium cauliflower (600 g)*

*1 cup (240 g) unsweetened vegan coconut yogurt*

*½ tsp harissa powder or paste (or leave out for young children)*

*Juice of 1 lime*

*1 (13-oz [370-g]) can chickpeas, drained*

*6 medium carrots, sliced lengthways*

*2 red bell peppers, roughly chopped*

*2 tbsp (30 ml) extra-virgin olive oil*

*1 clove garlic, unpeeled*

*4 oz (100 g) baby spinach*

*Small handful fresh mint leaves*

## TAHINI DRESSING

*⅓ cup (90 g) unsweetened vegan coconut yogurt*

*2 tbsp (30 g) light tahini*

*1 tbsp (15 ml) grade A maple syrup*

*Juice of ½ lemon*

## TO SERVE
*Leafy green salad*

# Warming Jerk Jackfruit with Pineapple, Corn, Peppers and Sweet Potato

Jackfruit is a very useful vegan alternative to meat. It's a versatile fruit that absorbs flavors well, making it ideal for savory dishes. You can buy it either in cans or vacuum packed. Here we have lightly coated the jackfruit with a little bit of delicious jerk spice and balanced the flavors with roasted pineapple, sweet potato wedges, corn on the cob and peppers. This sheet pan meal is a vibrant array of color and flavor. You can serve it straight from the tray, though our kids also like to load the pineapple, jerk jackfruit and peppers into tacos with fresh crispy lettuce, rice and black beans, eating the cobs and the wedges on the side.

SERVES: 4    PREP TIME: 10 minutes    COOK TIME: 45 minutes

1 (13.5-oz [380-g]) can jackfruit pieces in salted water

2 tbsp (30 ml) extra-virgin olive oil, plus more for drizzling

¼–½ tsp jerk blend spices (use ¼ tsp for younger children)

9 oz (260 g) pineapple chunks

2 large sweet potatoes, scrubbed and sliced into wedges

2 bell peppers, deseeded, roughly chopped

4 ears corn on the cob, each cut in half

TO SERVE (OPTIONAL)

Tortillas

Lettuce

Cooked rice and beans

Flatbreads (page 77)

Preheat the oven to 400°F/200°C (180°C convection) and line a large roasting pan or baking sheet with parchment paper.

Drain and pat dry the jackfruit with kitchen paper towels and slice the pieces in half. Add to a bowl with the extra-virgin olive oil and the jerk blend spices. Toss together until the jackfruit is covered. Spread the jackfruit out onto the baking sheet.

Arrange the pineapple pieces, sweet potato wedges, bell pepper and corn on the cob evenly around the jackfruit. Drizzle with extra-virgin olive oil and place the baking sheet in the center of the oven to bake for 25 minutes.

Remove the baking sheet from the oven and turn the sweet potato wedges and corn on the cob over. Return to the oven and bake for another 20 minutes until the corn on the cob turns golden.

Remove from the oven and serve either as-is, divided among plates, or in tacos with fresh crispy lettuce, with rice and beans or wrapped in flatbreads.

# Easy Baked Squash Risotto

We've made this soothing and crowd-pleasing Italian staple recipe easier than ever. Although stirring a risotto can be notionally therapeutic, we wanted to enjoy the satisfying nature of the dish without the physical time needed to make it, and so we have included this easy bake-in-the-oven risotto recipe. The flavor combination of roasted butternut squash and sage is one of our favorites when it comes to an unctuous risotto. We like to toast pine nuts to scatter over the top to serve, but if you don't have any in the cupboard, walnuts or almonds work equally well.

SERVES: 4   PREP TIME: 10 minutes   COOK TIME: 30 to 40 minutes

**To roast the butternut squash:** Preheat the oven to 400°F/200°C (180°C convection). Line a large baking sheet with parchment paper.

Peel the butternut squash, and slice into ¼-inch (1-cm)-thick rounds, before removing the seeds and slicing into small, cubed pieces. Spread the squash out across the baking sheet, drizzle over the extra-virgin olive oil, then scatter over the dried sage, salt and pepper and place in the oven to roast for 30 minutes.

**To make the risotto:** Meanwhile, in a large ovenproof cast-iron saucepan (with a lid), heat the olive oil over medium heat. Add the shallots and garlic and cook for 5 minutes until they start to soften. Then tip in the rice and mix well for 1 to 2 minutes, until the rice turns slightly translucent. Pour over the stock and add the nutritional yeast, dried sage, salt and pepper and stir. Place the lid on the saucepan and put in the oven to bake for 15 minutes. Then remove the pan from the oven, add half the butternut squash, stir, replace the lid and return it to the oven along with the remaining butternut squash on the baking sheet. Continue to cook for 8 to 10 minutes, until the rice is tender.

Toward the end of the rice cooking time, lightly toast the pine nuts in a dry skillet for 3 minutes until they turn golden. Keep them moving so that they don't catch and burn. Remove from the heat and set to one side.

Add the olive oil to the same skillet and bring to medium heat, then add the fresh sage leaves and fry for a few minutes until they turn slightly crispy. Remove the sage leaves from the oil and place onto a kitchen paper towel.

Once the squash is roasted and the rice is cooked, remove them both from the oven and stir the remaining roasted squash pieces through the risotto. Serve with a scattering of toasted pine nuts and the sage leaves, either whole or crumbled.

If there are any leftovers, allow the food to completely cool. Portion into airtight containers and store in the fridge for 24 hours or in the freezer. Defrost thoroughly before reheating.

## BUTTERNUT SQUASH

*1 medium butternut squash*

*2–3 tbsp (30–45 ml) extra-virgin olive oil*

*1 tsp dried sage*

*Pinch salt*

*Freshly ground black pepper*

## RISOTTO

*1 tbsp (15 ml) extra-virgin olive oil*

*2 shallots, finely chopped*

*3 cloves garlic, crushed and finely sliced*

*1½ cups (400 g) risotto rice*

*1½ quarts (1½ L) vegetable stock*

*3 tbsp (15 g) nutritional yeast*

*1 tbsp dried sage*

*½ tsp salt*

*¼–½ tsp freshly ground black pepper*

## TO SERVE

*2 tbsp (16 g) pine nuts*

*1 tbsp (15 ml) extra-virgin olive oil*

*Small handful fresh sage leaves (about 12)*

# Tomato, Pepper and Cannellini Bean Pasta Bake

This is a simple meal that we make frequently. It's a firm family favorite and is an ideal mid-week dish. Filled with comforting flavors, simple to prepare and freezer-friendly, it's also easy to hide a few more vegetables in if you feel the family needs a veggie boost. The creamy pasta is topped with melted vegan cheese, so there is nothing here that even the pickiest of eaters can argue with.

Although we usually make this dish with whole grain pasta, to boost the nutritious content we also regularly make it gluten-free by using pasta made from chickpea or lentil flour.

SERVES: 4    PREP TIME: 15 minutes    COOK TIME: 40 minutes

7 oz (approx. 200 g) dried whole grain pasta

1 tbsp (15 ml) extra-virgin olive oil

1 leek, finely sliced

1 celery stalk, finely diced

1 red bell pepper, roughly chopped

1 clove garlic, sliced

1 (14-oz [400-g]) can cannellini beans, drained

⅔ cup (160 g) unsweetened vegan coconut, almond or oat yogurt

Handful fresh basil

1 tsp dried Italian herbs

1 vegetable stock cube

2 (14-oz [400-g]) cans chopped tomatoes

⅔ cup (150 ml) boiling water

1 tbsp (15 ml) grade A maple syrup

¼ tsp salt

Freshly ground black pepper

1⅓ cups (150 g) grated vegan cheese

Preheat the oven to 400°F/200°C (180°C convection).

Bring a large saucepan of water to a boil and cook the pasta until al dente. Once cooked, drain and set to one side.

In a large saucepan, heat the oil over medium heat. Sauté the leek, celery and bell pepper for 5 minutes, until softened. Add the garlic and cook for another 4 minutes, stirring occasionally.

Tip in the cannellini beans and vegan coconut yogurt. Tear up and add the basil leaves, sprinkle over the dried herbs and crumble in the stock cube. Pour over the canned tomatoes, the boiling water and maple syrup. Lightly season with salt and pepper and stir through. Bring to a gentle simmer and cook for a further 10 minutes, then remove from the heat.

Stir the drained pasta into the tomato sauce and transfer everything into a large ovenproof dish, approximately 10 x 8 inches (26 x 20 cm). Evenly scatter the grated cheese all over the top and place the dish in the center of the oven. Bake for 15 minutes, until the sauce is bubbling and the cheese has melted. Remove from the oven and serve.

If there are any leftovers or you'd like to make a larger batch to freeze, allow the food to completely cool. Portion into airtight containers and store in the fridge for 2 days or in the freezer. Defrost thoroughly before reheating.

# Herby Sausage and Mediterranean Vegetable Bake

This simple dinner is easy to put together with minimal prep and then popped in the oven to cook. Finding a good vegan sausage alternative will always boost a dish; there are some tasty herby or Mediterranean-style smoked sausages that work particularly well in this dish.

We've used a variety of vibrant vegetables—mixed peppers, zucchini and eggplant. Everything goes into one pan and then the oven does all the work for you, roasting the ingredients to perfection. Any dish with sausages in it goes down very well with our kids (even the grown-up ones).

There are many ways to serve this dish or you can enjoy the flavors on their own. You may have pasta, rice or a large salad, but we love it the most with thick slices of toasted sourdough, rubbed with garlic and drizzled with extra-virgin olive oil.

SERVES: 4     PREP TIME: 15 minutes     COOK TIME: 60+ minutes

**To make the sausage and vegetables:** Preheat the oven to 400°F/200°C (180°C convection).

Pan-fry the sausages in a skillet with 1 tablespoon (15 ml) of oil until they are brown all over, then set aside.

Line a large baking sheet with parchment paper. Spread the onion, bell peppers, zucchini, eggplant, cherry tomatoes and cloves of garlic across it. Nestle the parcooked sausages in amongst the vegetables. Drizzle all the vegetables with 3 tablespoons (45 ml) of olive oil and season with salt and pepper. Place the baking sheet in the oven to cook for 40 to 50 minutes. Once baked, remove the baking sheet from the oven and scatter with the olives.

**To make the herby dressing:** Combine one of the roasted cloves of garlic from the baking sheet, the fresh parsley, basil, olive oil, capers and lemon juice in a small blender. Blend until you have a smooth dressing. Drizzle over the roasted vegetables and vegan sausages and serve.

## SAUSAGE & VEGETABLES

*8 vegan herb sausages or Mediterranean-style vegan sausages*

*4 tbsp (60 ml) extra-virgin olive oil, divided*

*1 large red onion, sliced*

*3 medium-size mixed bell peppers, cut into large slices*

*1 medium zucchini, cut into ½-inch (1-cm)-thick slices and then half-moons*

*1 small eggplant, chopped into 2-inch (5-cm) pieces*

*1¾ cups (250 g) cherry tomatoes, whole*

*4 cloves garlic*

*Pinch salt*

*Freshly ground black pepper*

*½ cup (90 g) green olives, pitted*

*Fresh parsley*

## HERBY DRESSING

*¼ cup (15 g) fresh flat-leaf parsley*

*¼ cup plus 2 tbsp (15 g) fresh basil*

*7 tbsp (105 ml) extra-virgin olive oil*

*1 tbsp (15 g) capers*

*Juice of ½ lemon*

# Warm Summer Salad with Roasted Peaches and Lentils

Salads can become repetitive. A lot of lettuce leaves, tomatoes and English cucumber, possibly with a few olives thrown in for luck—these don't really make for a satisfying meal. We decided that our summer-inspired salad needed to be a little different. It has slices of roasted peaches and new potatoes baked with a dusting of orange zest and thyme on a bed of lentils, creating the main structure for this wonderfully light and uplifting salad.

We love fresh herbs and, whether you have a windowsill or a dedicated herb garden, we'd thoroughly recommend keeping a small selection of herbs in pots to elevate the flavor of any meal. They are easy to grow and an ideal way to introduce children to the joy of growing their own vegetables. Mint, rosemary, parsley, basil and thyme are all worth the space and occasional watering, and all make a tasty addition to any salad, including this one.

SERVES: 4    PREP TIME: 10 minutes    COOK TIME: 40 minutes

17 oz (480 g) new potatoes or quartered potatoes

2 tbsp (30 ml) extra-virgin olive oil

Pinch salt

Freshly ground black pepper

2 (14-oz [400-g]) cans lentils, drained and rinsed

4 cloves garlic

6 peaches, pitted and quartered

Zest 1 orange

2 sprigs fresh thyme or 1 tsp dried thyme

10 stems tender stem broccoli

1 avocado, pitted and sliced

¼ cup (36 g) almonds, roughly chopped

TO SERVE

1 small English cucumber

1 medium zucchini

Juice ½ lemon

3–4 tbsp (45–60 ml) extra-virgin olive oil

Preheat the oven to 400°F/200°C (180°C convection). Line a large baking sheet or roasting pan with parchment paper.

Place the potatoes in a bowl, drizzle over the olive oil and sprinkle with salt and pepper. Tumble them around until covered. Tip them onto the baking sheet and place in the oven to roast for 20 minutes.

Remove the pan from the oven and carefully spread the lentils around the potatoes, then place the garlic and peaches, cut-side up, on the lentils. Zest the orange over the potatoes and place the sprigs of thyme in the pan. Return to the oven and roast for 10 minutes before adding the broccoli stems and cooking for a final 10 minutes.

While the broccoli cooks, make the salad by shaving long thin ribbons from the cucumber and zucchini using a vegetable peeler. Toss them together in a bowl with a good squeeze of lemon juice and a liberal drizzle of extra-virgin olive oil.

Finally remove the tray from the oven, scatter the sliced avocado and chopped almonds over the top, then serve with the ribbon salad.

# Homemade Takeouts

As the weekend draws nearer, we can lose the desire to cook and sometimes gravitate toward a takeout menu. So, we thought we'd entice you to create your own takeout menu to enjoy whenever you like. Whether that's during the week, entertaining friends and family, or when you don't want that bloated post-takeout feeling. We should have named this chapter "Fun Feasting" as the results are delicious and impressive. There are recipes here to ensure that you never feel short-changed eating plant-based, whether at a barbecue, a curry night or a fun-filled pizza evening.

Throughout this chapter, we have taken takeout favorites and turned them into your new plant-based takeout menu. There are the usual suspects—a great burger, curries and, of course, pizza. With our Quick Family Night Pizzas (page 119), these nights in our homes are family affairs, with the kids kneading the dough, shaping it and then everyone going crazy with the toppings—except for the one child who will always prefer a Margherita pizza and the odd fresh basil leaf.

Another of the children's favorites is the Sticky Smoked Barbecue Cauliflower Wings (page 126)—yes, cauliflower. Apparently if you cover it in a sticky barbecue sauce, they'll eat any unlikely vegetable.

These homemade takeout recipes are simple and some can be made ahead and frozen—making them perfect to pull out on a lazy Friday night when you know you want something particularly tasty, but don't have the energy to make it. Try the Thai Green Curry (page 120); we are slightly obsessed with it. Freeze a batch of it, then simply defrost, heat up, add some fresh herbs or a squeeze of lime juice and you are ready to go. Or you could keep the paste ready in the fridge, then simply add the vegetables and coconut milk.

If you are uncertain about introducing your children to curry, we would recommend the smooth and lightly spiced Creamy Vegetable Curry (page 112). It has been a favorite with our children as they have grown up and we can vouch for its child-friendly appeal. The spices are not hot or even warm—they just add a beautiful depth of flavor without the heat.

For plenty of other international dishes, look in Quick and Easy Mid-Week Meals for Tasty Meat-Free Balls with Spaghetti (page 61) or Zucchini and Pea Carbonara (page 69); in Batch Cooking, there is the Lentil, Coconut and Spinach Dahl (page 90), a Moroccan-Inspired Tagine (page 94) and our ultimate Three-Bean Chili (page 85), all of which never fail to hit the spot.

# Creamy Vegetable Curry

This is a truly creamy curry with a beautiful balance of flavors—perfect for introducing younger children to curries and at the same time being appreciated by adults' palates.

When our children were smaller, if a sauce had tiny bits in it, it was picked over and remarked upon and the enjoyment of the meal was lost, so we have blended this curry sauce until it is silky smooth. It still has all the same ingredients, it's just they will never know. Serve with flatbreads, rice and a dollop of yogurt. This recipe is great to batch cook and freezes really well.

SERVES: 4    PREP TIME: 10 to 15 minutes    COOK TIME: 30 minutes

*2 tbsp (30 ml) extra-virgin olive oil, divided*

*1 red onion, finely diced*

*2 cloves garlic, finely sliced*

*1-inch (2-cm) piece of ginger, grated*

*1 tbsp (5 g) ground cumin*

*1 tbsp (5 g) ground coriander*

*½ tsp turmeric*

*½ tsp ground cinnamon*

*½ tsp fenugreek seeds*

*5 whole cardamom pods, seeds removed and ground or ¼ tsp ground cardamom*

*1 tbsp (16 g) tomato puree*

*1 (14-oz [400-g]) can chopped tomatoes*

*¾ cup (180 ml) water*

*1 red bell pepper, chopped into bite-size pieces*

*1 zucchini, chopped into bite-size pieces*

*1 (14-oz [400-g]) can chickpeas, drained*

*⅔ cup (150 ml) unsweetened vegan coconut yogurt*

TO SERVE
*Flatbreads (page 77)*

*Rice*

*Unsweetened vegan coconut yogurt*

In a large pan, heat 1 tablespoon (15 ml) of oil over medium heat. Add the onion, garlic and ginger and fry for 5 to 6 minutes, until the onion starts to soften. Then add the cumin, coriander, turmeric, cinnamon, fenugreek and cardamom. Stir and cook through for a couple of minutes, until the spices become very aromatic and toasted. Then add the tomato puree, stir and cook for another couple of minutes.

Tip in the chopped canned tomatoes and water. Allow the sauce to bubble and simmer for 15 minutes and reduce down a little, stirring occasionally. Carefully spoon the sauce into a blender and blitz until it is silky smooth.

Meanwhile, add a little oil to a skillet over medium heat, then add the chopped red bell pepper and zucchini and cook for 8 minutes, until the vegetables start to soften. Now pour the smooth curry sauce over the vegetables and tip in the chickpeas. Stir and allow to simmer for 10 minutes. Finally stir in the coconut yogurt and gently cook for a couple of minutes. Serve with flatbreads or rice with additional yogurt.

Once the curry is completely cool, portion into airtight containers and store in the fridge for up to 2 days or freeze.

# Mushroom–Tofu Burgers

Who doesn't love a big juicy burger layered with slices of tomato, crunchy lettuce, burger garnishes and sauces? We love a vegan burger that is full of recognizable ingredients, so that there is a good bite to it, rather than a burger pretending to be meat. This tasty burger is made from a blend of mushrooms and tofu, with garlic, fresh herbs and a zingy lift from lemon zest on a delicious lightly toasted bun. Each of our children like to eat their burgers a slightly different way, so we add all the accompaniments onto plates and bowls for everyone to get creative and see who can make the biggest, sloppiest towering burger!

SERVES: 4 large burgers or 6 small patties    PREP TIME: 10 to 15 minutes    COOK TIME: 25 minutes

Drain the tofu in a sieve, then put it on a plate and use some kitchen paper towels to firmly press out as much excess liquid as possible.

Place a large skillet over medium heat and add a tablespoon (15 ml) of oil. Add the shallots and cook for 3 to 4 minutes, stirring frequently, before adding the mushrooms and garlic. Continue to cook for 8 minutes until the mushrooms have softened and the shallots are translucent. Then add the chives, stir and cook for another 2 minutes before removing from the heat. Set to one side to cool slightly.

Preheat the oven to 400°F/200°C (180°C convection) and line a baking sheet with parchment paper.

Crumble the drained tofu into small pieces and place in a large bowl. Add the cooled mushroom mix and the ketchup, soy sauce, flour, flaxseed, chia seed, lemon zest, salt and pepper. Stir together. Use your hands to form into four large burgers or six smaller patties about 1 inch (2 cm) high.

Return the skillet to medium heat and add the remaining tablespoon (15 ml) of oil. Fry the mushroom-tofu burgers on each side for 5 minutes, until they start to brown. Then carefully transfer the burgers to the lined baking sheet and place them in the oven to roast for 10 to 15 minutes, until they have browned.

Serve the burgers in lightly toasted buns with lots of lettuce, avocado, sliced tomato, pickles and your favorite sauces. These go well with sweet potato fries.

Place any remaining burgers on a plate, cover and store in the fridge for 24 hours.

## BURGER PATTIES

*10 oz (280 g) organic firm tofu*

*2 tbsp (30 ml) extra-virgin olive oil, divided*

*2 shallots, finely diced*

*10 oz (280 g) mushrooms, chopped into small pieces*

*2 cloves garlic, crushed*

*2 tbsp chives, finely chopped*

*2 tbsp (30 ml) tomato ketchup*

*2 tbsp (30 ml) soy sauce or tamari*

*2 tbsp (16 g) all-purpose flour (gluten-free if needed)*

*4 tbsp (40 g) ground flaxseed*

*2 tbsp (20 g) ground chia seeds*

*Zest of 1 lemon*

*Pinch salt*

*Freshly ground black pepper*

## TO SERVE

*Burger buns, lightly toasted*

*Crisp lettuce*

*Avocado, sliced*

*Tomato, sliced*

*Pickles*

*Vegan mayo*

*Tomato ketchup*

*Sweet potato fries*

# Pad Thai

There is a certain restaurant we like to go to that makes a seriously good vegan pad Thai, which is always hard to resist. We've always wanted to recreate this recipe at home and now you can, too. This pad Thai brings together a balance of soft rice noodles, crunchy bean sprouts, toasted peanuts, red bell peppers and silken tofu—with salty, sour, sweet and hot (if you like a little heat) flavors all in one intensely tasty and satisfying bowl of food.

SERVES: 4    PREP TIME: 10 to 15 minutes    COOK TIME: 20 minutes

SAUCE

4 tbsp (60 ml) tamarind paste

6 tbsp (90 ml) soy sauce or tamari

2 tbsp (30 ml) grade A maple syrup

Juice of 1 lime

2 tbsp (30 ml) rice vinegar

Pinch salt

PAD THAI

9 oz (250 g) flat wide dry rice noodles

½ cup (73 g) unsalted peanuts, roughly chopped

1 tbsp (15 ml) sesame or ground nut oil

1 leek, finely sliced

4 spring onions, finely sliced

2 cloves garlic, crushed and finely sliced

1-inch (2-cm) piece ginger, grated

1 red bell pepper, finely sliced

10.6 oz (300 g) organic silken tofu, drained

1 cup (100 g) bean sprouts

1 tsp dried chili flakes (optional)

1 red chili, sliced (optional)

¼ cup (4 g) fresh cilantro

GARNISH

2 spring onions, finely sliced

¼ cup (8 g) loosely packed fresh mint leaves, shredded

¼ cup (4 g) fresh cilantro

1 lime, cut into wedges

1 red chili, sliced

To make the sauce: In a small bowl, combine the tamarind paste, soy sauce, maple syrup, lime juice, rice vinegar and salt. Whisk until thoroughly combined and adjust ingredients to taste. Set aside.

To make the pad Thai: Prepare the rice noodles according to the package instructions.

Meanwhile, add the roughly chopped peanuts to a dry skillet and lightly toast for 3 to 4 minutes, until they turn golden. Keep the peanuts moving so that they do not burn. Remove from the heat and set to one side.

Pour the sesame oil into a large skillet or wok over medium heat. Then add the leek, spring onions, garlic and ginger and stir for 2 minutes. Now add the sliced bell pepper, silken tofu and bean sprouts. Stir, breaking up the tofu, until heated through.

Once the peppers are tender, add the noodles, sauce and the cilantro. Quickly toss the vegetables until all the ingredients are heated through. If the pad Thai seems a little thick, add a splash of water to loosen.

To serve, spoon the piping hot pad Thai into large bowls, then garnish by sprinkling over the peanuts, 2 finely sliced spring onions, the fresh mint and the cilantro leaves. Squeeze over the lime wedge and add chili flakes and fresh chili slices for those who will enjoy them.

# Quick Family Night Pizzas

We love pizza nights with all the family and with this quick, no-proof dough you can have all the fun without waiting. The kids can really be involved in kneading the dough, shaping their own individual pizzas and experimenting with toppings. The dough quantities in the recipe make enough for the adults to have a large pizza each and for the children to make their own small pizzas. We've included a super quick tomato sauce recipe, too, as we find the flavor and texture much better than store-bought versions, but if you are in a hurry, simply spread a little passata over the dough.

**SERVES:** 4 (10-inch [25-cm]) pizzas    **PREP TIME:** 30 minutes    **COOK TIME:** 10+ minutes

**To make the dough:** Sieve the flour into a large mixing bowl. Add the salt to one side and the yeast to the other. Make a well in the center of the flour, pour in the olive oil then gradually pour in the water. Bring the ingredients together with a wooden spoon until you have a rough dough.

Lightly flour the worktop and tip the dough onto the surface and knead for 10 minutes until the dough becomes smooth—get the kids to take turns.

Lightly oil the bowl and place the dough back into the bowl, cover and set to one side while you make the sauce.

Preheat the oven to 475°F/240°C (220°C convection).

**To make the tomato sauce:** Put the tomato passata, crushed garlic, basil leaves, salt and pepper into a blender and blitz until combined.

**To assemble the pizzas:** Tip the dough onto a lightly floured surface and divide the pizza dough into four equal pieces. Round these into balls. You can make four 10-inch (25-cm) pizzas or two large, roughly 12-inch (30-cm) pizzas and four smaller ones.

Use a rolling pin to roll the dough into roughly round or oval bases about ¼ inch thick (roughly ½ to ¾ cm). Slide each base onto the pizza trays or baking sheets. Sparingly spread the tomato passata over the base and sprinkle over a small handful of cheese and add your favorite toppings.

Place the trays in the top of the oven and cook the larger pizzas for 10 to 12 minutes and the smaller pizzas for 8 to 10 minutes, until the base is golden and cooked through.

Remove from the oven, slice into triangles, garnish with fresh basil and enjoy.

## DOUGH
*1 lb 2 oz (500 g) bread flour, plus more for dusting*

*2 tsp (10 g) salt*

*1 tbsp (12 g) instant dried yeast*

*4 tbsp (60 ml) extra-virgin olive oil, plus more to grease the bowl*

*1½ cups (360 ml) lukewarm water*

## TOMATO SAUCE
*7 oz (200 g) tomato passata*

*1 clove garlic*

*Small handful fresh basil*

*Pinch salt*

*Freshly ground black pepper*

## PIZZA TOPPING SUGGESTIONS
*2 cups (226 g) grated vegan cheese, either vegan mozzarella or cheddar or a mix*

*1 zucchini, thinly sliced*

*10 mushrooms, thinly sliced*

*½ cup (90 g) black or green pitted olives*

*1–2 tbsp (5–10 g) capers*

*1 red bell pepper, sliced*

*4 salad tomatoes, sliced*

## GARNISH
*Fresh basil*

# Thai Green Curry

One of our all-time favorite dishes has to be a really good Thai green curry. Blending the herbs and spices to create your own curry paste is incredibly satisfying and easy. This deeply rich curry is full of wonderful flavors, fragrant with fresh lemongrass and lightly spiced.

This is really a very versatile dish; once you have made the curry paste you can add any vegetables you might have in the fridge or freezer. Tofu or cooked new potatoes are a lovely addition, too. The paste will keep in a small jam jar in the fridge for a week and we'd recommend making a double batch of the paste so that you can freeze it into ice cube trays for a speedy mid-week dinner.

SERVES: 4, Makes ⅔ cup (200 g) paste     PREP TIME: 10 to 15 minutes     COOK TIME: 20 minutes

THAI GREEN CURRY PASTE

4 cloves garlic

1 large shallot, roughly chopped

2-inch (20 g) piece fresh ginger, chopped

2 stems lemongrass, roughly chopped

1 fresh green chili, seeds removed

1 tsp ground cumin

1 oz (30 g) fresh cilantro, roughly chopped

½ tsp tamarind paste

½ tsp galangal paste

3 kaffir lime leaves

Juice of ½ lemon or lime

3 tbsp (45 ml) extra-virgin olive oil or neutral oil

Pinch salt

¼ tsp freshly ground black pepper

**To make the curry paste:** Place the garlic, shallot and ginger into a food processor. Remove and discard the tough outer leaves of the lemongrass, then chop it into small pieces and add to the food processor along with the green chili, cumin, cilantro, tamarind paste, galangal paste, lime leaves, lemon juice, olive oil, salt and pepper. Blitz until all the ingredients combine and become a paste—we like it smooth. If necessary, scrape down the sides of the food processor to keep the ingredients moving.

(continued)

## FOR THE CURRY

*1 tbsp (15 ml) extra-virgin olive oil*

*5 spring onions, sliced*

*10 ears of baby corn, sliced in half*

*2 cups (150 g) sugar snap peas or green beans, sliced*

*8 stems tender stem broccoli*

*1 red bell pepper, sliced*

*1 (13.5-oz [400-ml]) can coconut milk*

*Fresh cilantro leaves*

*Juice of ½ lime*

## TO SERVE

*Brown or wild rice*

*Fresh cilantro leaves*

*Fresh chili slices (optional)*

*Chopped toasted cashew nuts*

**To make the curry:** In a large skillet over medium heat, heat the olive oil and fry the sliced spring onions for a couple of minutes before adding the baby corn, sugar snap peas, broccoli and bell pepper. Stir-fry the vegetables for 5 minutes.

Add 3 tablespoons (19 g) of the curry paste, stir it into the vegetables and cook for 4 minutes, then pour in the coconut milk. Stir, bring to a gentle bubble, reduce the heat and cook the curry for another 8 minutes, until the vegetables are tender. Finally, add some fresh cilantro leaves and squeeze in the lime juice.

Serve with rice, a scattering of cilantro leaves, chili slices (if using) and a sprinkle of toasted cashew nuts.

To store the curry, allow to cool fully and place in an airtight container in the fridge for up to 2 days or freeze in portion sizes. Store the paste in a sealed jam jar in the fridge for up to 1 week or freeze in ice cube trays.

# Bao Buns with Sticky Glazed Eggplant

Our children love these soft, chewy and slightly sweet steamed bao buns. They often help prepare the dough for the bao buns and then enjoy stuffing them with the flavorful filling of the smokey glazed eggplant and colorful crunchy vegetables. Making bread can sometimes feel a little daunting, but these little fun buns are straightforward and definitely worth making from scratch. It's another great way to get the kids involved in making a savory meal. We've used both a bamboo and metal steamer and they both work equally well, and you can tuck into the first batch while the second steams away. This is definitely a recipe that will impress guests.

SERVES: 4 (makes 8 bao buns)    PREP TIME: 25 minutes plus 3 hours rising    COOK TIME: 40 minutes

**To start the bao buns:** Line a large baking sheet with parchment paper. Sieve the flour into a large mixing bowl and add the yeast to one side and the salt, sugar and baking powder to the other. Then add the oil and unsweetened almond milk and gradually pour in the warm water and begin to stir together. As the dough begins to form, use your hands to bring it together into a ball then tip onto a lightly floured surface and knead for 10 minutes. The dough will become smooth.

Lightly oil a large mixing bowl and place the kneaded dough in the bottom, cover with a clean tea towel and leave in a warm place to rise for 2 hours.

Once the dough has doubled in size, tip it out onto a lightly floured surface and knead again for 2 minutes, knocking out the air. Then roll into a long log shape and divide into 8 equal balls.

Roll each ball out into an oval shape about ¼ inch thick (6 mm), 4.5 inches long (12 cm) by 3.5 inches wide (9 cm). Lightly brush the surface of each bun with oil, then lie a skewer (or similar) flat in the center of the oval and carefully fold the dough in half, and remove the skewer. Carefully place each folded bao bun onto the lined baking sheet. Cover the buns and leave to rise for another hour, until they have doubled in size.

While the bao buns are proving for the second time, start to make the eggplant filling.

(continued)

## BAO BUNS

*1¾ cups (225 g) all-purpose flour, plus more for dusting*

*1 tsp instant dried yeast*

*¼ tsp salt*

*1 tbsp (15 g) superfine caster sugar*

*½ tsp baking powder*

*1 tsp sunflower oil, plus more to oil the bowl and buns*

*2 tbsp (30 ml) unsweetened almond milk*

*⅓ plus 2 tbsp (105 ml) warm water*

# Bao Buns with Sticky Glazed Eggplant (Continued)

**To make the sticky glazed eggplant filling:** Preheat the oven to 400°F/200°C (180°C convection) and line a large baking sheet with parchment paper.

Cut the eggplant into strips, roughly 3 x 1.5 inches (7.5 x 4 cm). Add the eggplant strips to a large bowl and drizzle with the olive oil, salt and pepper. Pour over the teriyaki sauce and make sure all the eggplant is covered in the marinade.

Lay the eggplant strips onto the baking sheet and place in the oven to roast for 25 minutes.

**To steam the bao buns:** Place a large steamer with water (ideally with two tiers, if you have them) over medium heat and bring to a boil. Place a layer of parchment paper into the base of the steamer tiers and carefully use a large spatula to place the bao buns into the steamer. Leave a ½-inch (2-cm) gap between the buns. Reduce the heat and leave the buns to steam for 15 minutes, until they puff up. Remove the bao buns from the steamer and leave to cool slightly.

If making the bao buns in advance, steam, leave to cool fully, cover and chill in the fridge overnight. Steam for a couple of minutes before serving.

**To assemble:** Prepare the vegetables and when the bao buns have finished steaming, fill them with the eggplant, spring onions, bell pepper, carrot, cucumber, a sprinkling of sesame seeds and some fresh cilantro. Add some chili for heat, if desired.

## EGGPLANT FILLING

*1 medium eggplant*

*2 tbsp (30 ml) extra-virgin olive oil*

*Pinch salt*

*Freshly ground black pepper*

*4 tbsp (60 ml) vegan teriyaki sauce*

## TO SERVE

*2–3 spring onions, finely sliced*

*1 red bell pepper, finely sliced*

*1–2 carrots, grated*

*¼ cucumber, sliced into matchsticks*

*1 tbsp (9 g) sesame seeds*

*Fresh cilantro*

*1 red chili, sliced (optional)*

# Sticky Smoked Barbecue Cauliflower Wings

Dipping vegetables in a batter and then baking them with a sticky barbecue glaze is a lovely way to make eating vegetables more fun and delicious. Here, cauliflower is the star vegetable—yes, another way to get your family eating this brilliant veg. Once cooked, the florets are tender on the inside and deliciously sticky, with a slight crunch on the outside. For ease, we've baked the cauliflower florets instead of frying them. They are great for sharing just as they are or enjoyed as a side dish with the Mushroom-Tofu Burger (page 115) or as a tasty alternative filling for the Bao Buns (page 123).

SERVES: 4    PREP TIME: 20 minutes    COOK TIME: 30 to 40 minutes

## BARBECUE SAUCE
⅔ cup (160 ml) tomato ketchup

1 clove garlic, grated

⅓ cup plus 1 tbsp (90 g) light brown sugar

1 tbsp plus 1 tsp (20 ml) apple cider vinegar

1 tbsp plus 1 tsp (20 ml) soy sauce or tamari

1 tbsp plus 1 tsp (20 ml) vegan Worcestershire sauce

1 tsp smoked paprika

Pinch salt

Freshly ground black pepper

## CAULIFLOWER
1 head cauliflower

3 cups (324 g) bread crumbs (gluten-free if needed)

## BATTER
1 cup (125 g) all-purpose flour (gluten-free if needed)

1 cup (250 ml) unsweetened plant-based milk

2 tsp garlic powder

1 tsp onion salt

2 tsp smoked paprika

Pinch salt

Freshly ground black pepper

Preheat the oven to 400°F/200°C (180°C convection) and line a baking sheet with parchment paper.

To make the barbecue sauce: Add the ketchup, garlic, brown sugar, apple cider vinegar, soy sauce, Worcestershire sauce, paprika, salt and pepper to a saucepan. Whisk together and bring to a boil, then simmer for 15 minutes until it reduces and becomes a thicker sauce.

To make the cauliflower: Break the cauliflower into small florets. Then add the bread crumbs into a large bowl. Make the batter in a large bowl by whisking together the flour, plant-based milk, garlic powder, onion salt, paprika, salt and pepper. Coat each floret fully in the batter, shake off any excess batter, then coat in bread crumbs before placing on the baking sheet.

Place in the oven and bake for 20 minutes. Remove the sheet from the oven and generously brush each floret in the barbecue sauce (we like to coat half in the sauce and keep the other half crispy for dipping). Return the sheet to the oven and continue to bake for 15 to 20 minutes.

Serve the piping hot barbecue cauliflower wings with the remaining barbecue sauce.

# Cakes, Bakes and Desserts

In this chapter, we make sure that enjoying a plant-based lifestyle does not mean that your family has to miss out on special treats. We've created uncomplicated recipes for every season and occasion, whether you are looking for a show-stopping celebration cake or a decadent chocolate dessert. We feel it is important to know that you are never more than a few minutes away from biting into a cookie that's wonderfully chewy in the middle and crisp on the outside. We've also included recipes that make ideal additions to lunch boxes and are brilliant after-school snacks.

Cupcakes and muffins are one of the first baking experiences we shared with our children. This is where, as a parent, you have to leave behind your instinct to take control of everything, embrace the flying flour and dropped butter and appreciate that the dog/cat/hamster will end up with sticky fur because your little one doesn't quite understand the need to wash hands and not touch everything. It's all part of their learning experience. Take in a deep breath, and enjoy the satisfaction on your little one's face when the cakes come out of the oven—we all know that there should have been twelve in the batch, but if you achieve nine then you are doing well.

For this very reason, we've kept the recipes accessible and ingredients straightforward, so conjuring up a Chocolate Celebration Cake (page 138), Raspberry and White Chocolate Muffins (page 162) or a tasty Vanilla and Buttercream Birthday Cake (page 135) is as easy as one, two, three (well almost).

Baking is one of our favorite ways to unwind—we love to experiment, tweak classic recipes, mix up our favorite flavors like the Peanut Butter and Brownie Chocolate Chunk Cookies (page 131) or our latest "twist" on banana bread. Any scrumptious bake that leads to a moment of calm and a cup of tea, or can be made ready for friends arriving, is the perfect bake for us. The Almond Butter and Chocolate Chunk Banana Bread (page 152) and the savory Leek, Pea and Cheese Scones (page 156) are perfect for this.

Our dessert choices often change with the seasons, and for us, many desserts evoke a happy family and childhood memory, which is why when writing this chapter, we knew there were certain recipes that had to be included. For the warmer months, we have the amazing Summer Berry Meringues (page 141). Once you know how to make these beautiful meringues, you'll find you'll use the recipe alongside other desserts—the kids like them smashed with whipped cream and raspberries. There's also one of our children's favorites, the gorgeous No-Bake Lemon Cheesecake with Blueberry Compote (page 159)—there is always an argument over who gets the last piece. For the cooler months, you can entice your family with Sticky Toffee Pudding (page 151) drizzled with toffee sauce, and a Plum, Berry, Apple and Cinnamon Cobbler (page 144)—pure joyous comfort in a bowl.

# Peanut Butter and Brownie Chocolate Chunk Cookies

We have experimented with so many cookie recipes over the years. Our goals are to perfect the wonderful crackle top, balance the ratio of chocolate-to-dough and make the cookie chewy in the center but still slightly crispy on the outside. With these peanut butter and brownie cookies we've combined two of our favorite flavors and added extra chocolate chunks, just to make sure we've covered all bases. This is a great, no-fuss recipe for kids to have fun making, or for you to whip up to calm those cookie cravings. Enjoy every chewy cookie bite!

**MAKES:** 15 cookies     **PREP TIME:** 10 minutes     **COOK TIME:** 11 minutes

Preheat the oven to 350°F/175°C (160°C convection) and line a large baking sheet with parchment paper. Add the ground flaxseed to a small bowl with the water. Mix together and set aside.

Meanwhile, sieve the flour, cocoa powder, baking powder and baking soda into a medium mixing bowl. Add the chocolate chunks and stir together.

Combine the sugars and butter in a mixing bowl and stir thoroughly before adding the flaxseed mix, peanut butter and vanilla extract. Stir until smooth.

Now add the sugar-and-butter mixture to the dry ingredients and mix until you have a cookie dough.

Scoop a heaped tablespoon (about 1½ tablespoons' worth) of cookie dough into your hands and roll into a ball. Place, spaced out, onto the baking sheet. Flatten each cookie to about ½ inch (15 mm) thickness with your fingers. If using a large baking sheet, we recommend about 8 cookies to each sheet. Then place the sheet in the oven to bake for 11 minutes. The chocolate chunks will be melted and the cookies will have a slight crackle on top.

Remove the cookies from the oven and place the sheet on a cooling rack and leave for 10 minutes to enjoy a soft warm cookie or leave to cool completely.

Store cookies in a cool place in an airtight container for up to 3 days. The cookie dough can also be frozen. Before baking, defrost the dough then follow the above instructions to bake.

*1½ tbsp (15 g) ground flaxseed*

*3 tbsp (45 ml) water*

*1¼ cups (150 g) all-purpose flour (gluten free if needed plus ¼ tsp xanthan gum)*

*¼ cup (30 g) cocoa powder*

*½ tsp baking powder*

*½ tsp baking soda*

*½ cup (80 g) vegan dark chocolate, chopped into small chunks*

*½ cup (100 g) golden superfine caster sugar*

*½ cup (70 g) light brown sugar*

*½ cup (110 g) vegan butter, softened*

*⅓ cup (90 g) smooth or crunchy peanut butter (use a thick peanut butter)*

*1 tsp vanilla extract*

# Caramel Mini Bites

Here is a fun recipe for you all to get sticky fingers with. It's a delicious no-bake treat that tastes great whether it is made with small hands and rustic charm or with finesse. There is plenty of squashing and dipping fingers into melted chocolate to keep all ages occupied.

The base layer is an almond and vanilla no-bake biscuit, topped with a sweet gooey caramel. This is then left to firm up in the fridge before being covered in a final layer of smooth silky chocolate.

MAKES: 16 slices     PREP TIME: 40 minutes     COOK TIME: 1 hour

**BISCUIT LAYER**

*8 Medjool dates (about 150 g), pitted*

*1 cup (100 g) ground almonds*

*⅓ cup (30 g) desiccated coconut*

*1 tsp vanilla extract*

*1 tbsp (15 g) coconut oil, solid*

*Pinch salt (optional)*

Line the base and sides of an 8 x 4-inch (20 x 10-cm) loaf pan with parchment paper.

To make the biscuit layer: Place the pitted dates into a food processor and blend until they break up into a rough paste. Then add the ground almonds, coconut, vanilla extract, coconut oil and salt, if using and blend until the mix becomes a fine crumb and binds together when you squeeze some between your fingers.

Tip the biscuit base mix into the lined loaf pan and press firmly down, using a potato masher, your hands or the back of a spoon to form an even layer. Place in the fridge to chill while you make the caramel layer.

**(continued)**

# Caramel Mini Bites (Continued)

## CARAMEL LAYER

14 Medjool dates (about 250 g), pitted

½ cup (130 g) smooth cashew or almond butter

¼ cup (60 ml) light tahini

¼ cup (60 ml) grade A maple syrup

1 tbsp (15 ml) vanilla extract

## CHOCOLATE LAYER

5 oz (150 g) vegan dark or milk chocolate, broken into small pieces

1 tsp coconut oil

**To make the caramel layer:** Put the dates in the food processor and blend until they form a smooth paste. Then add the nut butter, light tahini, maple syrup and vanilla extract. Blend again until you have a smooth caramel mix. You may need to add a tablespoon (15 ml) of water just to loosen the mix if it is too thick.

Remove the base layer from the fridge and spoon the caramel mix on top, spreading it evenly and smoothing the surface. Return to the fridge to set.

**To make the chocolate layer:** Meanwhile, melt the chocolate and the coconut oil in a heatproof bowl over a bain-marie.

There are two ways to cover the caramel in chocolate. The first is to pour an even layer of the melted chocolate over the top of the chilled caramel and place in the fridge to set.

Then once set, remove from the fridge and the pan and use a warm knife (place the knife in a bowl of boiled water to heat up) to slice the slab into 16 pieces.

Alternatively—and a little messier, but undoubtedly more fun—remove the set caramel slab from the fridge and lift it out of the pan, then slice into bite-size pieces. Line a baking sheet or plate (that will fit in the fridge) with parchment paper. Now dip the caramel squares into the melted chocolate and rotate until they are fully covered. Carefully remove and place base-side down on the lined sheet. Repeat with the remaining caramel bites. Using a small spoon, drizzle any remaining chocolate in a zig-zag pattern over the pieces and then place in the fridge to set.

Store in an airtight container in the fridge for up to 4 days.

# Vanilla and Buttercream Birthday Cake

It's the kids' birthday and we all need a quick and easy birthday cake recipe up our sleeve that can be shared at parties with family and friends. This sheet cake has one layer of a light vanilla sponge, a vanilla buttercream icing and a scattering of chocolate chips or multi-colored sprinkles. Feel free to keep it simple or let your imagination have some fun and sculpt the sponge into whichever animal, mermaid or character your little one has their heart set on.

This is also an ideal recipe to get the children involved with—weighing, measuring and mixing ingredients are all really important skills and when the end result is a delicious cake, it makes it a lot more fun.

**SERVES:** 12 to 16     **PREP TIME:** 15 minutes     **COOK TIME:** 30 minutes

**To make the cake:** Preheat the oven to 400°F/200°C (180°C convection). Line the base and sides of an 8 x 8-inch (20 x 20-cm) square brownie pan with parchment paper.

Combine the milled flaxseed and water in a bowl and stir, then set to one side. In a separate bowl, combine the plant-based milk, apple cider vinegar and vanilla extract. Stir and set to one side.

In a mixing bowl, combine the butter and sugar then cream together. Stir in the soaked flaxseed mix and the plant-based milk mixture. The mix may curdle a little, but will come together once the flour is added and thoroughly mixed together.

Sieve the flour, xanthan gum (if using), baking powder, baking soda and salt into the mixing bowl and then stir together to combine thoroughly.

Pour the cake mix into the baking pan, gently smooth the surface of the cake then place in the middle of the oven. Bake for 30 minutes, until lightly golden on top. Insert a skewer or cocktail stick into the center of the cake, and if it comes out clean, remove the cake from the oven.

Place the cake in the pan on a cooling rack and allow to cool fully before removing from the cake pan.

### CAKE

*3 tbsp (45 g) ground flaxseed*

*6 tbsp (90 ml) water*

*¾ cup (180 ml) unsweetened plant-based milk*

*1½ tbsp (20 ml) apple cider vinegar*

*2 tsp (10 ml) vanilla extract*

*¾ cup (180 g) vegan butter, softened*

*¾ cup plus 1 tbsp (170 g) golden superfine caster sugar*

*1¾ cups plus 1 tbsp (230 g) all-purpose flour (use gluten-free flour if needed and add ¼ tsp xanthan gum)*

*1 tsp baking powder*

*½ tsp baking soda*

*½ tsp fine salt*

(continued)

# Vanilla and Buttercream Birthday Cake (Continued)

**To make the icing:** While the cake is baking, add the butter to a mixing bowl or use a stand mixer and mix until soft. Add the vanilla extract and gradually add the sifted confectioners' sugar a spoonful at a time until the sugar and butter are combined to make a smooth buttercream. If needed, add a tablespoon (15 ml) of plant-based milk to make the icing a little creamier. Food coloring can be added at this point to tint the buttercream if desired.

**To decorate:** Using a palette knife, generously spread the buttercream over the top of the cooled cake. Add your choice of decorations and serve.

Store the cake in an airtight container for up to 3 days.

## ICING

½ cup (115 g) vegan butter

1 tsp vanilla extract

2 cups (240 g) confectioners' sugar, sifted

1 tbsp (15 ml) plant-based milk (optional)

2–3 drops of food coloring (optional)

## DECORATION IDEAS

⅓ cup (50 g) vegan chocolate chips

3 tbsp (12 g) vegan sprinkles

Vegan chocolate flakes

# Chocolate Celebration Cake

We adore chocolate and find any excuse to make this, our favorite chocolate celebration cake. Marking special occasions with this statement three-tier rich sponge chocolate cake, decorated to impress, is utterly satisfying and completely indulgent. The sponge recipe is easy to put together, so much so that if it's the middle of the week and we feel like a piece of cake, we'll divide the recipe ingredients by three and bake a single layer of the sponge, possibly dust it with confectioners' sugar and savor a slice or two.

Your non-plant-based family and friends will have no idea that this cake is vegan, and the recipe works brilliantly as a gluten-free bake. We've used a beautiful alternative for making a plant-based icing (for a simple buttercream refer to the vanilla sheet cake icing recipe on page 137). As always, let your imagination run with the cake decorations. This may look a little grown-up but, believe us, once the kids get hold of the decorations, the cake takes on a whole new style.

SERVES: 10 slices     PREP TIME: 40 minutes     COOK TIME: 30 to 33 minutes

## CAKE FOR THREE TIERS

⅔ cup (160 ml) extra-virgin olive oil, neutral oil or coconut oil, plus more for oiling the pans

3¼ cups (400 g) all-purpose flour (use gluten-free flour if needed and add ½ tsp xanthan gum)

2 tsp (9 g) baking powder

1 tsp baking soda

1¼ cups (160 g) cocoa powder

¼ tsp salt

2 cups plus 1 tbsp (500 ml) unsweetened plant-based milk (we like to bake with almond milk)

1 cup (250 ml) hot water (boiled and slightly cooled)

2 tbsp (30 ml) apple cider vinegar

2 tsp (10 ml) vanilla extract

2¼ cups (500 g) muscovado sugar (or soft dark brown sugar)

**To make the cake tiers:** Heat the oven to 350°F/180°C (160°C convection). Line the base and sides of three 8-inch (20-cm) round springform cake pans with parchment paper and lightly wipe the sides of the pans with oil. If you only have one or two cake pans, you can bake the cake one layer at a time.

Sieve the flour, baking powder, baking soda, cocoa powder and salt into a large mixing bowl and stir together. In a separate mixing bowl, combine the plant-based milk, hot water, oil, apple cider vinegar, vanilla extract and sugar and stir together.

Pour the wet mix into the dry and stir to combine. Divide the cake batter evenly between the prepared cake pans. As the batter is wet, we'd recommend placing the cake pans onto a baking sheet to avoid any unexpected leaks (if your springform isn't as tightly sprung as it used to be). Place in the center of the oven and bake for 30 to 33 minutes. The cake is baked when you insert a skewer into the center and it comes out clean.

Remove the cake pans from the oven and place on a wire rack to cool for 30 minutes, then remove the sides of the cake pans and transfer to the wire rack to cool completely.

(continued)

## ICING

*4.5 oz (130 g) vegan dark chocolate, broken into pieces*

*⅔ cup (160 ml) vegan cream*

*¾ cup (165 g) vegan butter, softened*

*2¾ cups (335 g) confectioners' sugar, sifted*

*2 tbsp (11 g) cocoa powder, sifted*

## TO DECORATE

*4 oz (100 g) vegan chocolate flakes*

**To make the chocolate icing:** Add the dark chocolate pieces and vegan cream into a small saucepan. Gently melt together over low heat. Stir, remove from the heat and allow to cool slightly.

Add the softened butter to a large mixing bowl or stand mixer and beat until smooth. Gradually add the sifted confectioners' sugar and cocoa powder and continue to beat until combined and creamy. Now pour in the melted chocolate and cream mixture and cream together with the butter icing.

**To assemble and decorate:** Place a sponge layer onto a cake tray or plate. Then, using a palette knife, spread an even layer of icing to cover the top of the sponge. Place on the next sponge and ice. Finally place on the last sponge layer and evenly spread a thicker layer of the icing over the top of the cake. You may leave the decoration here and add some flaked pieces of chocolate. Alternatively, you could spread the icing around and down the sides of the cake and even pipe a pattern onto the top and fill the top of the cake with chocolate flakes.

The cake will store for up to 2 days in an airtight container.

NOTE: *In an ideal world we'd all have three springform cake pans that are the exact size, but even we don't, so either bake in rotation or it's unlikely anyone will notice if there's a ¼-inch (0.5-cm) difference in cake diameter.*

# Summer Berry Meringues

Meringues made with aquafaba are a revelation! They are incredibly light, sweet and surprisingly easy to make. Aquafaba is the name for the leftover liquid produced when cooking legumes and pulses, in this case we use aquafaba from a can of chickpeas, as it's the correct consistency for making these amazing crisp white meringues. Pop the leftover chickpeas in the fridge for later use.

Serve these meringues with whipped vegan cream and topped with sweet juicy strawberries, raspberries and blueberries. This is a very useful recipe to have and one you'll find you will make to complement other desserts. For instance, to add another dimension to the Chocolate and Ginger No-Bake Tart (page 148) make small meringues and place them on the top of the tart—this is a delicious addition!

SERVES: 8 nests and 12 kisses     PREP TIME: 1 to 2 hours to chill the aquafaba, plus 20 minutes
COOK TIME: 1 hour 15 minutes

Chill the aquafaba in the fridge for 1 to 2 hours or overnight before preparing the meringues.

Preheat the oven to 250°F/120°C (100°C convection). Line two large baking sheets with parchment paper.

Sieve the chilled aquafaba into a large, scrupulously clean mixing bowl. In a separate small bowl, mix the cream of tartar and the superfine sugar together.

Using either a stand mixer with a whisk attachment or a hand-held electric whisk on medium speed, whisk the aquafaba for about 5 minutes, until it starts to form soft peaks.

Now gradually add the sugar mixture, 1 tablespoon (12 g) at a time, making sure that each spoonful of sugar has dissolved before adding the next. Check by rubbing a little of the mixture between your fingers—it should feel smooth, not grainy. If it is grainy, keep whisking.

Continue until all the sugar has been used up. Then add the vanilla extract and whisk on high for another couple of minutes. The meringue mix should now look thick, glossy and form stiff peaks on the end of the whisk when turned upside-down.

(continued)

⅓ cup plus 1 tbsp (100 ml) aquafaba (liquid from a can of chickpeas)

¼ tsp cream of tartar

½ cup (100 g) superfine caster sugar

1½ tsp (7 ml) vanilla extract

# Summer Berry Meringues (Continued)

To make the meringue nests, spoon the meringue mix into a piping bag fitted with a round or star nozzle. Push any air out of the top of the piping bag and carefully twist it up at the end. To pipe the meringue nests, gently squeeze and pipe a spiral of meringue onto the baking sheet, starting at the center, until the circle is about 3 inches (7 cm) wide. Then pipe a double layer on the outer edge to create the nest shape.

To make the meringue kisses, gently squeeze the mixture onto the baking sheet and pull the bag up and away to make a peak. Repeat until you have used all the meringue mixture. We make about 8 meringue nests and 12 meringue kisses.

Place in the oven and bake for 1 hour and 15 minutes. Leave to cool for 10 minutes before carefully placing on a wire rack to cool completely. Enjoy with vegan whipped cream and berries.

Store the meringues in an airtight container for up to 3 days.

*Vegan whipped cream*
*1¼ cups (200 g) strawberries*
*¾ cup (100 g) blueberries*
*¾ cup (100 g) raspberries*

# Plum, Berry, Apple and Cinnamon Cobbler

We can't resist a warm, comforting and easy-to-make pudding. Crumble had always been our go-to autumn/winter dessert until we made our first cobbler. The beautiful flavors of the fruit, with the reassuring aroma of cinnamon, topped with a delicious cake-like cobbler, are heaven in a dessert bowl. The scent will have the family appearing in the kitchen, demanding a bowl long before it's ready to eat. We can be indecisive about what makes the best serving accompaniment to the sticky fruit cobbler, so we've given you a list of suggestions to enjoy.

SERVES: 6    PREP TIME: 15 minutes    COOK TIME: 30 minutes

## FRUIT LAYER

*8 plums*

*4 apples*

*1 cup (150 g) blueberries, blackberries or blackcurrants*

*1 tsp ground cinnamon*

*4 tbsp (60 ml) grade A maple syrup*

*2 tbsp (16 g) cornstarch*

## COBBLER TOPPING

*⅓ cup plus 1 tbsp (100 ml) unsweetened almond or oat milk*

*2 tbsp (30 ml) apple cider vinegar*

*1¼ cups (280 g) all-purpose flour (use gluten-free flour if needed and add ¼ tsp xanthan gum)*

*⅔ cup (140 g) golden superfine caster sugar, plus more for sprinkling*

*2½ tsp (11 g) baking powder*

*1 tsp ground cinnamon*

*⅔ cup (140 g) vegan butter, softened*

Preheat the oven to 400°F/200°C (180°C convection).

**To make the fruit layer:** Slice the plums in half, remove the stones and then cut each half into 4 pieces. Put these in a saucepan. Slice and remove the core from the apples, then chop the apples into roughly 1-inch (2-cm) pieces. Add these to the saucepan. Then tip in the blueberries, cinnamon, maple syrup and cornstarch and stir them into the fruit. Set the pan over medium heat and cook until the fruit starts to soften, stirring occasionally so the fruit doesn't stick to the pan (add a splash of water if this happens). This should take about 10 minutes.

**To make the cobbler topping:** Meanwhile, add the unsweetened plant-based milk to a small bowl, then spoon in the apple cider vinegar, stir and set to one side.

In a mixing bowl combine the flour, sugar, baking powder, cinnamon and mix together. Now add the softened butter and rub it through the flour with your fingers until the mix looks like fine bread crumbs. Then pour in the unsweetened almond milk mixture and stir until combined.

**To bake the cobbler:** Spoon the fruit mix into an ovenproof 9 x 7-inch (23 x 18-cm) baking dish and, using a large serving spoon, evenly dollop the cobbler mix on top of the fruit (roughly 8 cobbles), leaving a few narrow gaps between the cobbles to allow the fruit juices to bubble through. Sprinkle the top of the cobbler with some extra golden superfine sugar.

Place in the center of the oven and bake for 30 to 35 minutes, until the cobbler topping has risen and turned golden brown. Remove from the oven and serve on its own or with hot custard, vegan ice cream, yogurt or a drizzle of vegan cream.

Leave any leftovers to cool and either store in an airtight container in the fridge for 2 days or freeze in portion sizes.

# Quick Chocolate Orange Pots

The most unexpected meeting of ingredients creates these orange-infused, blissful little chocolate pots. We still haven't told the children that the chocolate orange pots they adore are made with silken tofu, because we know they would turn their noses up and refuse to eat them. The result of minimal prep and a handful of ingredients transforms into a smooth, silky dessert that feels completely indulgent.

---

MAKES: 4 (4-oz [140-ml]) pots     PREP TIME: 10 minutes

---

Drain the silken tofu in a sieve and set to one side.

Roughly chop the chocolate and place in a heatproof glass bowl. Either melt over a bain-marie or in 40-second intervals in the microwave. Allow the chocolate to cool for 5 minutes.

Now put all the ingredients in a high-powered blender or the small bowl of a food processor and blend them together until silky smooth and fully combined—this will take a few minutes.

Pour the mix evenly between the pots and either eat straight away or place in the fridge for an hour to firm up slightly.

Cover and store the chocolate pots in the fridge for up to 2 days. Remove the pots from the fridge 15 minutes before eating.

*10.5 oz (300 g) organic silken tofu*

*5.5 oz (150 g) good quality vegan chocolate (we use 70%+ cocoa solids)*

*4 tbsp (60 ml) grade A maple syrup*

*Zest of 1 orange*

*½ tsp orange extract*

# Chocolate and Ginger No-Bake Tart

This chocolate-lovers' dessert is no-bake and easy to make. The simple nature of this recipe means that it is the perfect sumptuous dessert for when you need to feed a crowd and impress your guests. We have an ongoing love affair with the flavor combination of chocolate and ginger. We've maintained a subtle hint of ginger in this dessert so that it is easier on younger children's palates. As they grow older, we recommend increasing the amount of ginger you include; for an adult palate we add 9 ounces (250 g) of dark chocolate and 1 ounce (25 g) of stem ginger. Simply savor each mouthful of the nutty no-bake tart base and the decadently smooth, creamy chocolate ganache filling.

Warning: The children will try to pinch the chocolate ganache mix, so be quick about pouring it and putting the dessert in the fridge to set.

SERVES: 10 slices      PREP TIME: for the base, 15 minutes plus 20 minutes to chill; for the filling, 10 minutes plus 1 hour to chill

## BASE

2 tbsp (54 g) coconut oil, plus extra for the pan

6 Medjool dates (about 120 g), pitted

1¼ cups (120 g) ground almonds

1 cup (90 g) desiccated coconut

½ oz (10 g) stem ginger in syrup

## FILLING

7 oz (200 g) vegan dark chocolate

1 cup (250 ml) coconut cream

3 tbsp (45 ml) grade A maple syrup

2 tbsp (30 ml) syrup from the jar of stem ginger

½ oz (10 g) stem ginger in syrup

1 tsp vanilla extract

## TOPPING

3½ oz (100 g) vegan 70%+ dark chocolate, finely sliced

**To make the base:** Carefully wipe a thin layer of coconut oil all over the sides and base of a 7-inch (18-cm) removable-bottom tart pan. We also like to line the base of the pan with parchment paper. In the bowl of a food processor, combine the coconut oil, dates, almonds, coconut and ginger for the base. Pulse until they form a rough crumb. Squeeze the mix in your hand. When it holds together, tip the mix into the lined and greased tart pan.

Using a potato masher, your fingers or the back of a spoon, firmly press the mix into the base of the pan. The base should be thin and even. Then, pressing with your fingers, use the remaining mix to mold the sides of the tart case. Place the base in the fridge to chill while you make the filling.

**To make the filling:** Chop the chocolate into small pieces and place in a heatproof bowl, then melt either using a microwave (in 40-second bursts) or in a bowl over a pan of simmering water—do not let the chocolate burn.

Then, in a blender or food processor, add the coconut cream, maple syrup, ginger syrup, stem ginger, vanilla extract and melted chocolate. Blend until the ingredients are smooth and fully combined.

**To assemble:** Remove the tart base from the fridge and pour in the filling. Smooth the surface with the back of a spoon and gently tap the pan on the countertop to help remove any trapped air bubbles, then lightly smooth the surface again. Place in the fridge to set for at least 1 hour.

Before serving, scatter the dark chocolate over the top of the tart.

Store in an airtight container in the fridge and consume within 3 days.

# Sticky Toffee Pudding

We cannot say the name of this dessert without a huge grin spreading across our faces. It is one of the ultimate family and crowd-pleasing desserts—one we have fond childhood memories of that our children now share.

This is our twist on this classic English pudding and one we had to succeed in transforming into a plant-based dessert. Sumptuous, gooey with sticky dates and a surprisingly light sponge, unapologetically covered in a sweet toffee sauce. And if you are indulging entirely (and we feel you should), the addition of a scoop of vegan vanilla ice cream, cream or custard will taste sublime.

---

SERVES: 6     PREP TIME: 10 minutes     COOK TIME: 35 minutes

---

**To make the pudding:** Preheat the oven to 400°F/200°C (180°C convection) and fully line an 8 x 8-inch (20 x 20-cm) baking pan with parchment paper.

Finely chop the pitted dates and put them in a small saucepan. Pour the unsweetened almond milk and water over them, then gently heat for 5 minutes, until the dates have softened. Remove from the heat and add the baking soda, vanilla extract and apple cider vinegar (it will fizz a little).

Meanwhile, in a large bowl, cream together the softened butter and sugars until smooth. Tip in the date mixture and molasses and stir into the creamed butter and sugar mixture. Sift in the flour and baking powder and fold together until thoroughly combined.

Now spoon the mixture into the prepared pan and place in the oven to bake for 35 minutes.

**To make the sauce:** In a small saucepan, melt the butter, sugar and vanilla extract together over medium heat; do not let it boil. When the sugar has dissolved, stir in the cream and bring the sauce to a simmer for 4 to 5 minutes, stirring continuously.

Remove the sticky toffee pudding from the oven, slice and serve drizzled generously with the toffee sauce.

Any leftover pudding can be kept in an airtight container for 2 days. Any leftover sauce can also be kept in the fridge for 2 days.

## PUDDING

12 Medjool dates (about 200 g), pitted

1 cup (250 ml) unsweetened almond milk

⅓ cup plus 1 tbsp (100 ml) water

1 tsp baking soda

2 tsp (10 ml) vanilla extract

1 tbsp (15 ml) apple cider vinegar

½ cup (120 g) vegan butter, softened

⅓ cup (60 g) light brown sugar

⅓ cup (50 g) light muscovado sugar

2 tbsp (40 g) molasses

1½ cups (200 g) all-purpose flour (use gluten-free flour if needed and add ¼ tsp xanthan gum)

2 tsp (9 g) baking powder

## TOFFEE SAUCE

⅓ cup (80 g) vegan butter

¾ cup (160 g) light muscovado sugar

2 tsp (10 ml) vanilla extract

⅔ cup (160 ml) vegan cream

# Almond Butter and Chocolate Chunk Banana Bread

No kitchen should be without a banana bread recipe; we find the baking of a banana bread both cathartic and satisfying. The scent that fills the kitchen and the familiar process of baking a recipe we make more regularly than we care to admit always makes us very happy indeed.

We also love having a delicious purpose for the overly ripe and squidgy bananas that the children refuse to eat. By using them to create a naturally sweetened bake with little added sugar, we are making the most of what would otherwise be food waste. Banana bread could be breakfast, a snack or a dessert; just cut into thick slices and enjoy.

SERVES: 2 lb (900 g) loaf     PREP TIME: 10 minutes     COOK TIME: 50 minutes

¼ cup (70 ml) unsweetened plant-based milk

1 tbsp (15 ml) apple cider vinegar

2 tbsp (20 g) ground flaxseed

6 tbsp (90 ml) water

1¼ cups (150 g) all-purpose flour (use gluten-free flour if needed and add ¼ tsp xanthan gum)

2 tsp (9 g) baking powder

1 tsp baking soda

1 cup (100 g) ground almonds

⅓ cup (60 g) golden superfine caster sugar

12 oz (350 g) bananas (weighed with skin on, roughly 3 medium bananas), mashed

1 tsp vanilla extract

¼ cup (60 ml) sunflower oil, olive oil or neutral cooking oil

¼ cup (60 ml) grade A maple syrup

2 tbsp (30 g) almond butter

⅔ cup (100 g) vegan dark or milk chocolate chips or chunks

1 oz (30 g) vegan chocolate, melted, for the swirl

Preheat the oven to 350°F/175°C (160°C convection) and line the base and sides of a 2-pound (900-g) loaf pan with parchment paper.

In a small bowl, pour in the plant-based milk and apple cider vinegar, stir and set to one side. In a separate small bowl, mix together the ground flaxseed and water and set aside.

Sieve the flour, baking powder and baking soda into a large mixing bowl. Then add the ground almonds, sugar, mashed bananas and vanilla extract and mix. Pour in the almond milk mix and flaxseed mix, sunflower oil, maple syrup and almond butter to the dry ingredients and carefully stir together. Then add the chocolate chunks and stir through. Spoon the mix into the prepared loaf pan.

Drizzle the melted chocolate over the top of the loaf. Use a skewer or cocktail stick to swirl the chocolate up and down the cake mix. Place the loaf in the middle of the oven and bake for 50 minutes until golden on top.

Allow to cool in the pan for 20 minutes, then transfer to a wire rack. Serve warm or at room temperature.

Keep the banana bread in an airtight container and eat within 3 days.

NOTE: We like to mix the flours we bake with and often include teff or buckwheat flours—keep half all-purpose flour and make up the rest of the weight with one of these flour alternatives.

# Fig, Orange and Cranberry Granola Bars

These handy, nutritious, no-bake granola bars are packed with juicy dried fruits and nourishing seeds. Because they are ready to grab and enjoy on the go, they are ideal for adding to lunch boxes or as an after-school snack. The base for these energy-boosting bars is a mix of dried figs and desiccated coconut. We've added pumpkin seeds and sunflower seeds along with juicy sweet cranberries and orange zest. We have, for ease, suggested pressing the mix into a pan to create bar shapes, but feel free to allow little hands to mold into cookie shapes or balls—or let them loose with the cookie cutters. For an added treat, drizzle with melted white chocolate.

MAKES: 8 slices    PREP TIME: 15 minutes    COOK TIME: 1 hour

Line a 9 x 4½-inch (22 x 11.5-cm) pan with parchment paper.

Put the figs and orange zest in the bowl of a food processor and blend until the figs become a smooth paste. Then tip in the chia seeds, walnuts, flaxseed, sunflower seeds, pumpkin seeds, coconut, cranberries and vanilla extract and pulse until the mixture is still a little rough—giving the final bar a little bite. For a smoother texture, continue to blend until the desired texture is reached.

Then tip the mix into the lined pan. Press the mix firmly down with the back of a spoon—we like to use a potato masher, this works really well. Place in the fridge to chill for 1 hour and then slice, drizzle with melted white chocolate, if desired, and serve.

Store in an airtight container at room temperature, or in the fridge if the kitchen is warm, for up to 5 days.

*1 cup (150 g) dried figs, roughly chopped*

*Zest of ½ orange*

*1 tbsp (10 g) chia seeds*

*⅓ cup (40 g) walnuts, chopped*

*2½ tbsp (25 g) flaxseed*

*⅓ cup (45 g) sunflower seeds*

*⅓ cup (50 g) pumpkin seeds*

*½ cup (50 g) desiccated coconut*

*½ cup (50 g) dried cranberries*

*1 tsp vanilla extract*

SERVING SUGGESTION
*Melted vegan white chocolate*

# Leek, Pea and Cheese Scones

These little savory scones are beyond delicious; eat them as they are or as an ideal accompaniment to a bowl of homemade soup. They are a tasty afternoon snack or great to take on picnics. Include them in your lunch box or enjoy them as a savory breakfast. Eat the scones warm or cool and spread with vegan butter or a thick layer of vegan cream cheese. This is definitely another recipe to get your youngsters involved with to show them that baking does not always have to be sweet and that savory bakes are equally satisfying and fun to make.

MAKES: 25 small scones    PREP TIME: 20 minutes    COOK TIME: 14 to 16 minutes

1 tbsp (15 ml) extra-virgin olive oil

1 medium leek, finely chopped

⅔ cup (90 g) frozen peas

¾ cup (180 ml) unsweetened almond milk

1 tbsp (15 ml) apple cider vinegar

1¾ cups (345 g) all-purpose flour (use gluten-free flour if needed and add ½ tsp xanthan gum)

4 tsp (18 g) baking powder

Pinch salt

⅓ cup plus 1 tbsp (85 g) vegan butter, cold and cut into cubes

1 cup (110 g) grated vegan cheddar cheese, divided

Preheat the oven to 400°F/200°C (180°C convection) and line a large baking sheet with parchment paper.

In a nonstick skillet, heat the olive oil over low to medium heat. Add the leek and sauté for 5 minutes, until it has softened. Remove from the heat and set aside.

Meanwhile, put the frozen peas in a heatproof bowl, cover them with boiling water and leave for 4 minutes. Drain the peas and set aside.

Pour the unsweetened almond milk into a small bowl, add the apple cider vinegar, stir and set aside as well.

Sieve the flour and baking powder into a large bowl and add a pinch of salt. Add the cubes of butter and rub in with your fingers until the mixture resembles bread crumbs. Now add the cooked leeks, peas and grated vegan cheese (reserving ¼ cup [20 g] of cheese for the top). Stir until combined evenly into the flour and butter.

Make a well in the center of the dry ingredients and pour in the almond milk mix. Bring the dough carefully together until the dough just comes away from the edge of the bowl; do not over handle the dough as this will make tough scones.

Turn the dough onto a lightly floured surface and gently flatten it with your hands until it is about 1 inch (2.5 cm) thick. Using a 2-inch (5-cm) fluted round cutter, cut the dough into approximately 25 scones, gently reshaping the dough as necessary.

If using a larger fluted round cutter, cook the scones for an extra 2 to 3 minutes.

(continued)

# Leek, Pea and Cheese Scones (Continued)

*2 tbsp (30 ml) unsweetened almond milk*

*½ tsp vegan Worcestershire sauce*

Make the glaze in a small bowl by combining the almond milk and Worcestershire sauce. Carefully place the rounds onto the lined baking sheet and brush the top of each one with the glaze mixture. Sprinkle the top of each scone with the remaining cheese. Place the baking sheet in the middle of the oven and bake for 14 to 16 minutes, until lightly golden.

Remove from the oven and place on a cooling rack. Enjoy the scones warm or cold.

Store in an airtight container for up to 2 days or freeze and defrost fully before eating.

# No-Bake Lemon Cheesecake with Blueberry Compote

We love the simplicity of this recipe—the smooth creamy texture of the lemon cheesecake layer on top of the firm chocolate and almond base, all topped with sweet sticky blueberries. It is a delectable, taste bud–tingling combination. We've reduced the amount of sugar that would normally go into a cheesecake recipe and none of the family have noticed. The soft lemon flavor is a lovely way to introduce children to citrus desserts—and this is the ideal dessert for sharing with all your family and friends. There is some chilling time to negotiate, but often, making a dessert in stages gives you time to create other recipes. It is also ideal if you are planning ahead for a family get-together and don't want to be rushing around on the day. This cheesecake is definitely worth the wait—and if there is any left over, we can guarantee our boys will try to sneak it for breakfast.

SERVES: 6     PRE-SOAK TIME: 4 hours or 30 minutes     ACTIVE PREP TIME: 45 minutes
BASE CHILL TIME: 30 minutes     SETTING TIME: 6 hours or overnight

To soak the nuts for the cheesecake: **Add the cashew nuts to a small bowl and then pour cold water over them so that it fully covers all the nuts. Cover and set to one side to soak for 4 hours. If you are in a hurry, pour boiling water over them and leave to soak for 30 minutes. The longer you leave the cashews to soak, the creamier the cheesecake will be.**

To make the base: **Lightly grease the base and sides of a 6-inch (16-cm) removable-bottom cake pan with coconut oil or vegan butter, then cut a circle of parchment paper to neatly line the base of the pan.**

**In the bowl of a food processor, add the coconut oil, dates, almonds, cacao powder and vanilla extract, then blitz until it turns into a fine crumb. The base mix is ready when you can squeeze it in your hands and it binds together. Tip the mix into the base of the cake pan and use the back of a spoon to firmly press it down into an even layer about ½ inch (1 cm) in depth. Place in the fridge to chill for 30 minutes.**

(continued)

½ cup (65 g) cashew nuts

SMOOTH CHOCOLATE BASE
2 tbsp (30 g) coconut oil, plus more to grease the cake pan

8 Medjool dates (150 g), pitted

1¼ cups (120 g) ground almonds

⅓ cup (40 g) cacao powder

1 tsp vanilla extract

# No-Bake Lemon Cheesecake with Blueberry Compote (Continued)

To make the lemon cheesecake layer: While the base is in the fridge, drain the cashew nuts and rinse them in water, then add to a high-powered blender (if you do not have one, use a food processor). Now add the vegan cream cheese, confectioners' sugar, lemon zest and juice and vanilla extract. Blend until the mix is smooth and silky.

To assemble: Remove the base from the fridge and pour the lemon cheesecake filling over it. Using a spoon, spread the mix until it is level, then give the base of the pan a gentle tap or two on the countertop to remove any trapped air bubbles. Level the surface, cover with a plate and place in the fridge to set for 6 hours.

To make the lemon and blueberry topping: In a small skillet, combine the maple syrup and blueberries and heat gently over medium heat. Add the lemon juice and cook until the berries start to sizzle and the juices turn slightly sticky—this should take about 8 minutes. Set aside to cool and to thicken slightly.

To serve: Remove the lemon cheesecake from the fridge about 10 minutes before serving. Then carefully remove it from the pan. Place onto a plate and spoon the blueberries over the top. Slice and serve.

Cover and store in the fridge for up to 2 days.

## LEMON CHEESECAKE LAYER

1⅓ cups (300 g) vegan cream cheese

¾ cup (100 g) confectioners' sugar

Zest and juice of 1 lemon

½ tsp vanilla extract

## LEMON AND BLUEBERRY TOPPING

2 tbsp (30 ml) grade A maple syrup

1⅓ cups (200 g) blueberries

Juice of ½ lemon

# Raspberry and White Chocolate Muffins

We all need a handy, quick and easy muffin recipe. This recipe has a sweet vanilla muffin base and includes raspberries and white chocolate, a flavor combination that all our children love. The recipe is easy for small hands to help with and straightforward enough for older children to make themselves. These are particularly popular with the children as the muffin is delicious, light and still slightly sticky when baked. We haven't included an icing, but if you would like to add a buttercream swirl to the top, use the buttercream icing recipe on page 137.

MAKES: 12      PREP TIME: 10 minutes      COOK TIME: 35 minutes

2 cups (250 g) all-purpose flour (use gluten-free flour if needed and add ¼ tsp xanthan gum)

2½ tsp (11 g) baking powder

1 cup (200 g) golden superfine caster sugar

½ cup (130 ml) sunflower oil or other neutral oil

¾ cup (180 ml) unsweetened plant-based milk

2 tsp (10 ml) vanilla extract

1¼ cups (150 g) fresh or frozen raspberries

7 oz (200 g) vegan white chocolate chips or chopped chocolate

Preheat the oven to 400°F/200°C (180°C convection) and line a muffin tin with 12 muffin papers.

In a large bowl, mix together the flour, baking powder and sugar. In a separate bowl, whisk together the sunflower oil, plant-based milk and vanilla extract.

Tip the frozen raspberries and white chocolate into the flour mix and stir through. Make a well in the center of the dry mix, pour in the wet ingredients, and fold together. Be careful not to overmix; it's okay if there are a few small floury lumps.

Spoon the mix evenly between the muffin papers, filling to three-quarters full. Place the muffin tin into the center of the oven and bake for 35 minutes, until golden brown. For an even coloring, bake the muffins for 20 minutes and then rotate the tin for the final 15 minutes. Check if the muffins are fully cooked by inserting a toothpick or skewer; it will come out clean when ready.

Remove the muffin tin from the oven and place on a cooling rack for 15 minutes. Then remove the muffins onto the rack to cool fully.

Store in an airtight container for up to 3 days.

# Acknowledgments

It has taken a long-lasting friendship and an unexplainable understanding of each other for us to write this book. Cooking for most people can be a singular activity (people get in the way and underfoot in the kitchen), but for us it has turned from a hobby into work life, teamwork and now this unexpected book.

It is safe to say that this book would not have been possible without the constant support of our families and long-suffering friends, who have heard nothing other than cookbook mutterings from us for months!

So, to our husbands, Pete and Nick: Thank you, we've done it now, it's safe to come out of hiding and, yes, we'll make you some new dishes. Thank you for believing in us when self-belief isn't our strong point.

To our gorgeous guinea pigs, our kids Aaron, Luca, Daniel, Matilda and Louis: Thank you for tolerating us as we've repeatedly asked try this, make this, don't do that and the constant call of I'll be there in a minute (for us to not appear). Your mothers are back, so you'd better pick up that washing.

To our parents, Jill and Peter, Monica and Martin: Thank you for letting us rant from a distance and reassuring us that we can do this. This was written in the times of COVID-19.

To Simon and Gina: Thank you for helpfully living in the U.S. and answering our queries about language, temperature and ingredient differences.

To Heather, Nick, Amber and Leo: We are unbelievably glad you are home and thank you for testing and eating our recipes.

And to our kitchen woof, Smudge: The long walks you took us on to clear our heads were invaluable.

WE LOVE YOU ALL SO MUCH!

And now, to Zoe: Thank you, you're an absolute super star. You've read every word, helped with our spirits and tweaked our language to make sense.

To Emma, Ruth, Emily, Beth, Anita, Sarah, Helen and Chloe: Thank you for always being there—you are all utterly gorgeous.

A huge thank-you to the kind loan of the amazing ceramics from the talented creatives at Fire Station Square Pottery—your work helps lift our food from the page.

Clearly a massive thank you to Sarah Monroe and the team at Page Street Publishing Co. for believing in what we do and giving us the opportunity to write our first cookbook. It is safe to say we have learned so much and loved every word (almost).

And lastly, but by no means least, to you our Healthy Twists community for supporting us for so long, for buying, reading and cooking recipes from this book. Making them in your kitchen and sharing the meals you create with your family and friends—you cannot imagine what a magical feeling that is for us.

From the bottom of our hearts, thank you.

# About the Authors

Claire Swift (on the left of the photograph) is from beautiful North Yorkshire, England, and spent a fun childhood scrambling around her grandma's garden in the Dales, with her sister and parents. After leaving school, Claire gained a BA Hons and an MA in landscape architecture in Leeds, where she continued to develop her love of creative design, plants and photography. On qualifying, Claire moved to the North West where she met her husband, Pete, and lives surrounded by the rolling countryside in Cheshire with their children, dog and ducks.

Sarah Biagetti (on the right of the photograph) is from the stunning historic city of Bath in the South West of England. After gaining a BA Hons degree in art history and anthropology in Oxford, she moved to London. There she first worked with authors, developing writers' tours, projects and collaborations across the world before working in the arts and sciences, developing innovative projects in the UK. Sarah moved to Cheshire with her husband over fifteen years ago, where they still live with their two sons.

Claire and Sarah share a love of the outdoors, yoga, running, long walks, great reads, cookbooks and mouthwatering food.

Claire and Sarah set up Healthy Twists five years ago to help families find an easy way to introduce and enjoy more plant-based meals, firmly placing vegetables and plants at the center of every table. Their award-winning blog has led them on quite an adventure, including appearances on TV programs, features in magazines, spots on podcasts, opportunities for demos at events, and writing and creating content for brands and clients. This is their first cookbook.

Read more on www.healthy-twists.com and follow along on social media @healthy_twists.

# Index

We invite you to join *The Plant-Based Family Cookbook* community on
social media! Check out the Healthy Twists Facebook group
and find us on social media:

📷 @healthy_twists

🐦 @Healthy_Twists

📌 @healthytwists

Tag your photos with recipes you've created from this book.
#HealthyTwistsFamilyCookbook

For more recipes and content from Claire & Sarah,
visit www.healthy-twists.com